Stuff and Consciousness:
Connecting Matter and Mind

Stuff and Consciousness: Connecting Matter and Mind

Toby Pereira

First published in the United Kingdom in 2014 by
Toby Pereira

ISBN 978-0-9929091-0-9

Produced by The Choir Press

Contents

Preface

I first got into thinking about consciousness and how it might arise from the brain when I was at school. A boy in my year recounted some interesting thought experiments on the subject, and I later recognised these when I read *The Mind's I* – a book of essays edited by Douglas Hofstadter and Daniel Dennett (1981a). The one story that stood out to me at the time was 'The Story of a Brain' by Arnold Zuboff. My brother Oliver was also into the subject and we had many discussions on it.

However, educationally, I did not take the philosophical route to begin with. I started off doing a degree in mathematics with physics, which soon became just mathematics, but then dropped the whole thing altogether and did a degree in psychology, which is a little bit closer to the philosophy of consciousness.

In the final year of my psychology degree, one of the courses I took was Scientific Studies of Consciousness taught by Kyle Cave. Up until that point my interest in the subject had been largely based on talking to a few people and my own thoughts on the subject. It was at this point that I started to read properly on the subject.

The following year I did a Master's degree in Philosophy of Mind: the only year I have spent doing philosophy in academia. In this year I had many other interested and interesting people to discuss ideas with, as well as all the relevant literature, and I was able to start ironing out my own thoughts on the subject of consciousness. For various reasons, I did not pursue a PhD, so that was the end of the line in terms of formal academic study. However, my interest in the subject did not wane and I decided to use the ideas from my essays and turn them into a book: this book, which you will hopefully enjoy. So I am writing this book as an academic outsider, but you should not find it lacking because of this. There's only one way to find out if my book really is lacking, and you've come this far.

Consciousness is a big enough problem that people from several academic disciplines want to be the one to 'solve' it and have claimed it as their subject. Philosophy, psychology, biology, neuroscience, computer science and artificial intelligence, and even quantum physics are all candidates for getting the job done. But where is the answer truly going to come from? Obviously I am writing this with my philosophy hat on, but contributions to the solution could come from various areas, and a full answer may well come from a combination of ideas from many different fields.

I've read books and articles by many people from these different fields, but possibly the three that have most influenced this book are philosophers Daniel Dennett, David Chalmers and Arnold Zuboff. Dennett and Chalmers are two of the biggest names in the general consciousness field anyway, and have both written on quite a wide range of topics within the philosophy of consciousness. You'll probably notice their influence, as I refer to their ideas on many of the topics I cover myself.

There are many people who have helped me write this book in various ways, whether it be by having a few discussions in the pub or reading a draft of this book. In alphabetical order, I would like to thank the following:

Catherine Annandale, Jenny Booth, Kyle Cave, Harriet Evans, Ross Field, George Graham-Pereira, Jacob Graham-Pereira, Oscar Graham-Pereira, Joe Hudson, Elizabeth Lovely, Tom MacDonald, Denis McManus, Nick Parkins, Emily Pereira, Heather Pereira, Noel Pereira, Oliver Pereira, Liz Philpott, Graham Pitts, John Revill, Simon Riches, Mark Snellgrove, Adam Strudwick, Nigel Tam, Matthew Wentworth, Oli West.

Part 1
Foundations

Chapter 1

Introduction

What Is Consciousness?

The study of consciousness is not some obscure branch of philosophy or neuroscience, but something that most people have surely considered at some point in their lives. You have it; I have it; a cat has it; an ant possibly has it; a bacterium possibly doesn't have it; a pen doesn't have it. This is a quick intuitive view on which things possess consciousness and which don't. Maybe you agree. Maybe you disagree. But you probably have an opinion. So in a way, it is surprising that books on consciousness are not more mainstream, as the subject is quickly accessible. Indeed, your own complex and nuanced conscious experiences automatically make you an expert before you even start reading.

The problem of consciousness has baffled philosophers for centuries, but why has something that seems so natural and obvious caused such a problem? And since it has, why isn't everyone talking about it? The nature of your very self is at stake. Seventeenth-century French philosopher René Descartes, often known as the father of modern philosophy, famously coined the phrase *Cogito ergo sum* – I think, therefore I am – as a starting point from which to draw other conclusions. He used his thinking – his consciousness – as proof of his existence. But what exactly is consciousness and what is its problem that has occupied so many minds over the centuries?

Without further delay, I will define the term 'consciousness' as I will be using it. To have consciousness is to have thoughts or feelings, or to experience. 'Consciousness', for our purposes, is defined in terms of how a being feels, rather than how it functions, so you cannot necessarily tell if something is conscious by studying its functioning and behaviour. For you to be conscious means that there is something it is like to be you, as American philosopher Thomas Nagel explains in his famous paper 'What is it like to be a bat?' (1974). When you ask someone or something what an experience was like, their answer only has real meaning if you are asking a conscious being. It was not like anything if they are not conscious.

Possibly the most common way of putting the problem of consciousness is in the guise of the 'Mind–Body Problem': how the body (specifically the brain), which is apparently purely physical, can give rise to the conscious mind, which consists of thoughts and feelings, and so does not appear to be obviously physical.

Have you ever considered the possibility that you are the only person who has real thoughts and feelings, and that everyone around you is just behaving as they do without actually having them, like mindless robots? I think most people have probably thought about this at some point in their lives. This conundrum is known as the 'Other Minds Problem', and the view that you are the only conscious being is known as 'solipsism'. If you have considered this, you have taken the important step of separating the two concepts of consciousness and brain function, and you should understand what the problem of consciousness is about. However, I am often surprised by the number of people who haven't really considered this and need the problem of consciousness explained to them. To me, it is one of the most obvious things in the world to wonder about.

All sorts of thoughts and feelings, whether they be seeing colours, feeling pain, thinking complex thoughts or experiencing emotions, are part of conscious experience. Consciousness is not just higher-level thoughts or self-awareness. If an animal experiences any sort of pain, for example, it is conscious too. There is no reason I can think of for saying that consciousness is unique to humans. Some may say that it is not present in most animals as they do not display any evidence of having self-consciousness (or self-awareness), such as recognising themselves in a mirror (see e.g. Gallup, 1970). But this is a separate, and I would argue vaguer, concept or class of concepts, roughly corresponding to consciousness of one's own self or one's own consciousness. If you punch an animal in the face and it experiences pain, then it is conscious. I am not going to get involved in a discussion of exactly what may or may not count as self-consciousness, but plain, bog-standard consciousness would exist in the smallest of life-forms if it had any subjective experiences at all.

In terms of self-consciousness, it is worth pointing out that you cannot ever be consciously aware of all of your conscious experiences, however counterintuitive that may sound. You may be consciously aware of the blue sky you are looking at, but you are not necessarily consciously aware of your own awareness of the blue sky. It is possible that you are, sitting there thinking about your own conscious thoughts, but this has to stop somewhere. No-one could ever be conscious of their entire consciousness, as it would lead to an infinite regress. Each thought about a conscious state would require the existence of a further thought to include that thought and so on, ad infinitum. So while it is possible to be self-conscious to a degree, no-one can ever be fully self-conscious in this sense.

American philosopher David Rosenthal (e.g. 2002) argues that a mental state is only conscious if you are aware of that state. This is known as the Higher-Order Thought or HOT theory of consciousness. This theory avoids the infinite regress because the awareness of the conscious thought (this awareness being the higher-order thought) does not have to be conscious itself. It can be an unconscious thought, but its existence is what makes the original thought conscious. The higher-order thought can be a conscious thought itself, but only if there is a further thought (a third layer) about that thought.

There is a body of literature on this theory, which I will bypass, but I don't think it holds up to scrutiny. It's not the contemplation that you are in pain that makes the pain hurt. Less cognitively advanced animals as well as very young children probably don't have the capacity to dwell that much on their thoughts and feelings, but I don't see this as a reason to say that they cannot be in conscious pain. Also, when you scan your eyes around the room, you take in a lot of visual information. I would argue that you are conscious of what passes through your visual field, albeit briefly, but you are unlikely to form higher-order thoughts about all of that. I will return to this topic briefly in chapter 7 when I've covered more of the relevant ground to look at it in a bit more detail.

Since you can never look upon your entire consciousness, there might be things that would surprise you about your own consciousness. It might not be as it seems to be! American philosopher and possibly the biggest name in the field of consciousness, Daniel Dennett, gives a good example of this regarding wallpaper that consists of many identical portraits of Marilyn Monroe, in his book *Consciousness Explained* (1991).

> It seems to you as if you are actually seeing hundreds of identical Marilyns. [...] What is not the case, however, is that there are hundreds of identical Marilyns represented in your brain. Your brain just somehow represents *that* there are hundreds of identical Marilyns, and no matter how vivid your impression is that you see all the detail, the detail is in the world, not your head.[1]

Consciousness and self-consciousness are separate concepts. And while you may possess self-consciousness about some of your consciousness, it is not a requirement for consciousness itself, and there is no guarantee that your self-consciousness gives a complete or accurate insight into your consciousness.

Psychological and Phenomenal Consciousness

The term 'consciousness' can be used in various ways in different walks of life, and we must be careful not to confuse vague everyday usage with our strict philosophical sense of the term. For example, when someone is said to lose consciousness after a head injury, they may still retain certain conscious thoughts (for example, if they are dreaming), so they would not be unconscious from our point of view.

Australian philosopher and one of the biggest names in the field, David Chalmers (1996), distinguishes between what he calls phenomenal and psychological mental states. Phenomenal mental states are states that are actually experienced. They are the conscious states that we are concerned with explaining in this book. Psychological mental states are the states involved in functioning and

---

[1]   p. 355, italics in original

behaviour. They are the states that cause things to happen in the physical world. As he explains:

> On the phenomenal concept, mind is characterized by the way it *feels*; on the psychological concept, mind is characterized by what it *does*. There should be no question of competition between these two notions of mind. Neither of them is *the* correct analysis of mind. They cover different phenomena, both of which are quite real. [...] At this early stage, I do not wish to beg any questions about whether the phenomenal and the psychological will turn out to be the same thing.[2]

As mentioned earlier, phenomenal states cover all of our experience, which has a lot of variety, including seeing colours, emotions, and complex thought processes. Anything that you consciously experience is a phenomenal state.

Chalmers adds that these phenomenal states do not exist in a vacuum and are always associated with a psychological state. This seems quite reasonable, since phenomenal states are most often considered to be a result of physical brain activity. On the other hand, until we find out how the physical/consciousness link works, we cannot rule out the possibility of phenomenal states that exist independently of anything physical or psychological.

But to take Chalmers's point, the phenomenal state of seeing green, for example, must have a psychological counterpart, or also simultaneously be the psychological state, or we would not talk about it, since it is the psychological state that is involved in functioning and behaviour. This also applies to beliefs; I mention this example because later on I talk about why people believe in consciousness and discuss this under the possibility that consciousness does not exist. It is conceivable for a psychological belief in consciousness to exist without there being any consciousness. I am sure you can see that in order for the discussion to make sense, it is important to distinguish between psychological and phenomenal belief.

---

[2]   pp.11–12, italics in original

To be clear, the distinction between phenomenal and psychological can be made at the level of consciousness itself, not just certain specific states:

> 'Consciousness' can also be used to refer to a variety of psychological properties, such as reportability or introspective accessibility of information. We can group psychological properties of this sort under the label of *psychological consciousness*, as opposed to the *phenomenal consciousness* on which I have been concentrating.[3]

American philosopher Ned Block (1995) uses the terms 'phenomenal consciousness' and 'access consciousness'. He uses phenomenal consciousness in the same way as Chalmers (it is standard in the literature), and his use of access consciousness largely corresponds to Chalmers's psychological consciousness, and is widely cited in the literature, but it appears to be a subset of psychological consciousness, as it's not as widely defined. It refers more to states that we have explicit access to and can refer directly to, rather than any states involved in functioning and behaviour. In this book, I will be using Chalmers's term 'psychological consciousness'.

The short story 'An Unfortunate Dualist' by philosopher Raymond Smullyan (1981) shows quite well what it means to separate psychological and phenomenal consciousness. The story is used to demonstrate the absurdity of this separation and specifically the absurdity of epiphenomenalism. He explicitly mentions dualism (to be covered in chapter 3, but essentially the view that consciousness is not physical) rather than epiphenomenalism, but it is more specifically epiphenomenalism, a subset of dualism, that the story is about. Epiphenomenalism is the view that (phenomenal) consciousness has no bearing on functioning and behaviour, and indeed no physical effects whatsoever; it is just an impotent by-product of the brain's physical processing. Epiphenomenalism is discussed at length in this book, and I do not brush it aside as simply as Smullyan does, as you will see.

In the story, there is a man who lives his life in pain for which there is no cure. He wants to die, but for various reasons does not

---

[3] p. 26, italics in original

want to commit suicide. Then along comes a drug that can destroy someone's phenomenal consciousness but leave the body and brain functioning exactly as before. To anyone on the outside, the drug would appear to have no effect whatsoever, but the man would lose all phenomenal consciousness and would experience nothing more. So the man decides to take the drug. But the night before he does so, his friend injects him with the drug while he is asleep to put him out of his misery. However, the man, with no phenomenal consciousness, still takes the drug the next morning. Yet he still reacts angrily, even after this double dose, as if the drug has not worked, and claims that he is still suffering.

Why does this happen, assuming that the drug does actually work? It is because in the world of this story, the psychological and phenomenal are separate. The man's phenomenal consciousness has been wiped out, leaving the psychological consciousness intact. He loses his phenomenal consciousness after the first dose from his friend. But he still has the same psychological beliefs as before, and behaves in exactly the same way as if the drug did nothing. This is why he still injects himself the next morning and goes on to react angrily. He still has the psychological belief that he is phenomenally conscious, both after his friend injects him with the drug and after he injects himself. Everything about his behaviour is indistinguishable from how it would be had he not taken the drug. But he has no phenomenal consciousness. Smullyan uses this story as a demonstration of how ridiculous he thinks epiphenomenalism is. However, it is not necessarily as simple as that, as you will see by reading on, when I discuss epiphenomenalism in detail from chapter 3. But my purpose in mentioning this story here is to demonstrate what it means to have a separate phenomenal and psychological consciousness.

Normally we would talk about consciousness in the phenomenal sense, but it is important to make the distinction, even though it may seem strange to talk about a consciousness that isn't really conscious. That is to say that psychological consciousness is not defined as 'consciousness' in the strict sense in which we are using the term, although it could still turn out to be one and the same as phenomenal consciousness, as it seems Smullyan is implicitly arguing. Phenomenal consciousness is the primary subject matter of this book and if I use the term 'consciousness' without any qualifier, it is phenomenal consciousness that I am talking about.

The Easy and Hard Problems of Consciousness

Trying to find out how a human brain functions is a very big problem itself, but it is conceptually distinct from the problem of consciousness. I say *conceptually* distinct because there are people who think that the problem of consciousness will fall away once the problem of functioning (psychological consciousness) is solved, so they may not be distinct in practical terms. But we can form separate concepts of them and they are defined differently, even if they turn out to be the same problem.

David Chalmers calls these the 'easy' problems and the 'hard' problem of consciousness. The easy problems are problems of functioning and behaviour. It is not that they are easy to solve as such, but that solving them is a case of learning more about the physical processing of the brain and doing neuroscience in the way that we are already doing. Following this path, we should one day learn why we behave the way we do, to any amount of detail. We will learn why someone says that they like the colour green and why they say they are conscious, as well as where their creativity and intelligence come from, all in physical terms. Solving the easy problems will tell us everything about psychological consciousness. And this is a case of scientists carrying on doing what they are doing, presumably with no big conceptual leaps required.[4]

However, all of this will not necessarily tell us anything about phenomenal consciousness. And this is what Chalmers means by the hard problem of consciousness. Granted, solving the easy problems would tell us why we insist that there is this hard problem of consciousness (as it would explain everything that we physically say or do), but that is not enough on its own. It is the actual conscious experience itself that we need to understand. We need to understand how the third-person physical world can give rise to the first-person

---

[4] Although see the discussion on the causal completeness of physics in chapter 3.

world of experience. Intuitively, it is difficult to see how solving the easy problems will answer this without any extra work being needed. There is a lot of debate as to whether the hard problem will simply disappear after solving all the easy problems, or indeed whether there really is a hard problem at all, and this will be discussed at length in chapters 3 and 5.

Another common way of outlining the hard problem of consciousness, coined by philosopher Joseph Levine (1983), is to say that there is an explanatory gap between physics and consciousness.

A Note on Qualia

A particular conscious feeling is often called a 'quale', but it is more often used in the plural, which is 'qualia'. This term is frequently used in the discussion of consciousness, when people talk about, for example, the redness of red or the hurt of pain. But Dennett (e.g. 1988; 1991, pp. 369–411) disputes the use of this term. He uses various examples to effectively show that these supposed qualia are not the elemental untouchable units of experience some believe them to be. He uses, as an example, the acquired taste of beer (e.g. 1988, pp. 60–61; 1991, pp. 395–396). Is it that a beer drinker gradually comes to like the quale he experiences when tasting beer, or does the quale itself change? Dennett's point is that there is no stand-alone quale that is independent of the rest of your experience. When you taste beer, you have certain experiences, and it is impossible to draw a line and cut off which part of the experience is the quale of the taste of beer and which is your opinion of that taste. This can lead to disagreement between people over whether the taste of beer changes over time or whether they start to like the same taste.

'Qualia' is not a term I use in this book, apart from in reference to other people's work. I wouldn't go so far as to say that the term is useless, more that it needs to be used with caution.

The Problem

While discussion of human brains clearly comes up a lot in this book, the problem is larger than that. The wider problem of consciousness is how the interaction of physical matter *in general* can give rise to consciousness. This includes the case of human brains, of course, but also other physical objects that may be conscious, such as animal brains, computers, aliens, and much more besides. I will also be questioning the link between the physical and consciousness. It may not seem a problem to you that the interaction of physical matter can give rise to subjective feelings, but it is my job to show you that it is a problem. Hopefully I will be able to convince you to see the problem in a new light.

What would it mean to solve the problem of consciousness? We would need to find exactly what governs the existence of consciousness, and the manner in which it governs. Essentially, we need to fully understand the nature of the relationship between physical matter and consciousness, if there is one. We need to know why a particular physical event causes a particular conscious experience. If there is no relationship between matter and consciousness, we need to know what consciousness does depend on, if anything, and the exact manner in which it does. It might be as complex as the laws of physics that govern the universe. It might even be more complex, but on the other hand it might be much simpler.

I should point out here that I do not solve the problem of consciousness in this book. You won't finish this book knowing everything that there is to know about consciousness, unless you work it out for yourself in the meantime. However, if that's what you require, I don't think you'll find what you're looking for in any book that currently exists. What I hope to do is gain some ground and point you in the right direction. By discussing other people's viewpoints and my own ideas, and by assessing various possible theories on the subject and their plausibility, it should become clear by the end of this book where I think we should be looking.

Some Readings

This book does not assume any prior knowledge on the subject of consciousness, and you should be able to follow the explanations and arguments even if this is the first thing you have read on the subject. However, there are some good introductory books available.

Introducing Consciousness by David Papineau and Howard Selina (2000) is part of a wider *Introducing* series of books on many subjects, and it gives a good grounding on the subject. However, I wouldn't pay too much attention to the last page, where it seems to give up the fight. *Conversations on Consciousness* by Susan Blackmore (2005) is a series of conversations between Blackmore and about twenty top names in the field, where they each outline their own perspectives and theories on the subject. This is a very useful tool for getting a feel for the wide range of theories that the subject yields. Obviously you can then look up the works of each of these people to get a more in-depth understanding of their ideas. *The Mind's I* (edited by Daniel Dennett and Douglas Hofstadter, 1981) is a collection of essays by various people, each followed by Dennett's and/or Hofstadter's own reflections on the essay. The essays aren't all in an academic style, and some take the form of stories. They are not all explicitly about consciousness, but it is the central theme. You might find some chapters to be more relevant than others, but it is a very interesting and eclectic book.

Chapter 2

Functionalism and the Uniqueness of Brains

Functionalism

It might seem obvious that consciousness would have had to evolve to help us to live in our environment, in order for us to have complex thoughts and make decisions. A being that functions unconsciously would surely not do very well in situations where higher cognitive powers are required. Indeed, we often talk about our more mundane and repetitive tasks as having been done unconsciously, but never say the same of novel or complex situations we encounter. But is consciousness itself actually required for dealing with these? Perhaps exactly the same physical processes could occur, and with the same functional effects, but without subjective experiences. What does consciousness itself do? Can consciousness and functioning (psychological consciousness) be separated or does consciousness automatically come with this level of functioning? And what exactly is *this* level of functioning?

If it is complexity of functioning that results in consciousness, then perhaps there is a level of complexity below which there is no consciousness. I think most people would agree that humans are conscious. But then we have to consider progressively less and less complex brains and systems. Is a chimpanzee conscious? A dog? A rat? An ant? A bacterium? A thermostat? A rock? Does consciousness come on like a light when processing is complex enough, or is consciousness something that exists to a lesser and lesser extent in all these beings and systems? If consciousness is a gradual thing, does this mean that a thermostat is conscious, if only to a small degree?

The view that everything has consciousness to some degree is known as 'panpsychism'. If consciousness comes on like a light, there would have to be a being with no consciousness that would suddenly become conscious with the smallest of increases in cognitive power.

Maybe it isn't simply complexity of functioning that is the issue. Perhaps there is something else that determines whether a being is conscious, something that has nothing to do with complexity of functioning. There are many people, including American philosopher John Searle, whose work I will be discussing in more detail later in this chapter, who think that complexity is not the issue, and that an 'intelligent' digital computer could never be conscious, however intelligent it became and however complex its processing.

The idea that consciousness is determined by functioning is known as 'functionalism'. Under this view, the precise physical make-up does not matter, as long as all brain functions are equivalently performed in some way. Under this view, an alien with a very different brain make-up still might have similar experiences to you when subjected to the same stimuli, known as the 'multiple realisability' of conscious states. If there were a being with a brain functionally equivalent to yours – for example, each neuron and its role is represented, although it could be constructed in a different way – it would be guaranteed to have exactly the same conscious thoughts. One could also consider a slightly larger part of the system than a neuron, and as long as each such part of a being's brain performed the same role as the equivalent part in your brain, then the two brains would still arguably be functionally equivalent. It's debatable how large this part could be, and what would count as a 'functional element', however (see discussion of Blockhead below).

Under functionalism, phenomenal consciousness would always correspond to psychological consciousness in a consistent manner. Opposing functionalism can in some cases give rise to the possibility of zombies. In philosophical circles, a zombie is a being that functions and behaves exactly like a human but has no consciousness at all, such as someone who has taken the consciousness-destroying drug in Raymond Smullyan's story (discussed in chapter 1). Sometimes it is used in a slightly weaker sense to mean a being that is simply not conscious, and not necessarily functionally equivalent to a human. The two similar but different uses of the term can lead to confusion, but I will be careful to use the term only in the strictest sense. To be clear, a zombie must be functionally and behaviourally equivalent to a human being. If it is not the functional state that produces consciousness, then someone could be in an identical functional state to you, and behave in the same manner, but have different conscious experiences, or perhaps even have none at all and therefore be a zombie. Of course, denying functionalism does not commit one to embracing the possibility of zombies, and this would depend on the specific theory.

One might assume that consciousness necessarily exists in the presence of more complex processing, such as in human brains, but you can't actually see consciousness in others, so there is no direct proof for this assumption. You can experience your own consciousness first-hand, but can only observe the behaviour of others, and then infer that they are also conscious, as they are beings physically and behaviourally similar to you. But you cannot prove outright that they have conscious thoughts, certainly not with our current levels of knowledge. This is why the Other Minds Problem exists. It is important to note that there is currently no physical evidence for the existence of phenomenal consciousness, and the idea that there could ever be is ridiculous to some people. My own views on the matter will become clear in due course (specifically in chapter 5).

The idea of functionalism was possibly behind the invention of the Turing Test, by British mathematician and computer scientist Alan Turing (1950). Taking part in the Turing Test are a computer and a human, as well as an interrogator to judge them. It is the computer's and the human's job to each convince the interrogator that they are the human. The interrogator asks the human and the computer questions, and receives a typed reply for each question, and at the end has to say which is the human. If the computer takes the test several times and is picked as the human on at least 50% of occasions, then it has passed, because the interrogators could not reliably distinguish between the human and computer.

The Turing Test is not limited to computers. It can be used on anything capable of producing written output. The question Turing set out with when devising the test was 'Can machines think?' but it can be modified to 'Are computers capable of conscious thought?' The way Turing used the word 'think' implied that he meant conscious thinking.

However, using the Turing Test as a measure of consciousness would be assuming a form of behaviourism (known as 'logical behaviourism') rather than functionalism, as two systems could be behaviourally identical (and thus perform identically in the Turing Test) but functionally different. Logical behaviourism says that any two beings that behave identically in response to the same stimuli would have the same consciousness, whereas according to functionalism, the internal processing would have to be equivalent. There is more to functionalism than a being saying it is in pain and therefore being in pain.

To give an example of the difference between the two stances, Ned Block (1981) came up with the idea of a giant look-up table to govern the behaviour of a being known as 'Blockhead'. In this look-up table, every input has a stock output response. If such a table were big enough (it doesn't matter if it would require more matter than is in the universe, being a thought experiment), then it could govern a being for its whole life without running out of responses. This being could be behaviourally identical to a human, but would not be functionally identical. In practice, however, any being that behaves like a human is likely to have similar internal functioning, but there could still be significant differences, even if not as great as the differences between a human and Blockhead. This is another demonstration that you cannot see consciousness in others, which further fuels the Other Minds Problem. At the other end of the scale, someone paralysed with locked-in syndrome may be incapable of any behavioural responses to stimuli, and so behaviourally indistinguishable from even a rock. This would not mean that the rock shared their conscious experiences.

Under functionalism, I would define a 'functional element' to be the largest part of a system that can be replaced with a behaviourally identical part with no change in consciousness. Therefore no relevant (in terms of consciousness production) functioning happens inside a functional element. The brain is not a functional element because it cannot be replaced with the behaviourally identical Blockhead, whereas a neuron might be. For this book, I am going to assume that if something can play the behavioural role of an individual neuron, then a brain made of these parts would be functionally equivalent to a human brain. I'm not going to spend too much time worrying about exactly what size a functional element would be, however.

The Turing Test was an inspired idea and could be useful in some situations, but it is no acid test for consciousness, as it seems to let behaviourism slip in through the back door. It would also throw out a computer or alien that is not human enough, as well as a non-human animal, as they would not be able to pass for a human in the test. I do not think there are many people who consider logical behaviourism to be a realistic theory of consciousness, in any case.

Functionalism seems a more realistic theory than logical behaviourism, as it is based on the equivalence of all the internal processing rather than just the behavioural result, and it is a commonly held view within consciousness studies. But this isn't the end of the story.

What (If Anything) Makes Brains Special?

In this section I will be discussing some of the arguments that have been made against the idea that consciousness is purely based on functioning, and what else it could be that endows brains with their consciousness.

Chinese Room

John Searle (e.g. 1981, 1998) uses his famous Chinese Room argument in an attempt to refute functionalism. His view is that no level or type of functioning can make a digital computer conscious. According to Searle, digital computers blindly manipulate symbols, and so the output, while meaningful to the operator, means nothing to the computer. With us humans, on the other hand, our behaviour and functioning obviously do mean something to us and don't require a separate operator to be meaningful.

Searle compares a computer to a person sitting inside a room who is given questions in Chinese, which are being passed through a hole.

The person in the room understands no Chinese, but he has instructions, written in English, explaining what to do with the Chinese writing; for example, if he sees a particular set of symbols (which, unbeknownst to him, mean 'What is your name?'), he is to copy out another set of symbols in response (which, unbeknownst to him, represent his name in Chinese). Following the instructions leads him to produce the output, which is also in Chinese, although he still has no understanding of it. He passes the written output back out through the hole. So it is possible for someone outside the room to have a conversation with the Chinese Room, in Chinese, despite there being no-one in the room who understands Chinese. Searle says that there is no understanding of Chinese in the Chinese Room and, analogously, there is no understanding in a digital computer.

The practical limitations of this thought experiment, such as the enormous timescale that would be involved and the size of the instruction manual, are not of importance. It is a thought experiment based on logical possibility and deserves to be taken at face value.

On the face of it, Searle's argument looks quite reasonable. It seems that there must be more to human understanding than blind symbol manipulation. There are arguments against Searle's position, however. The Systems Argument (e.g. Hofstadter, 1981a) says that while the man in the room doesn't understand Chinese, the system as a whole does. Saying that the man doesn't understand Chinese would be like saying that a particular neuron in a Chinese person's brain doesn't understand Chinese. The man is just one component of the system, even if he is a large and complex part.

In response to this, Searle (1981) suggests that the man could then memorise all of the rules and do away with the written instructions. Then there is nothing in the system apart from him, and yet he still doesn't understand Chinese. However, the man's brain could be seen as having two subsystems, one that understands Chinese and one that does not. Searle then goes back to base and argues that this still makes no difference to whether it is conscious as it is still just blind symbol manipulation, which cannot be conscious:

> The whole point of the original example was to argue that such symbol manipulation by itself couldn't be sufficient for understanding

Chinese in any literal sense because the man could write 'squoggle squoggle' after 'squiggle squiggle' without understanding anything in Chinese. And it doesn't meet that argument to postulate subsystems within the man, because the subsystems are no better off than the man was in the first place; they still don't have anything even remotely like what the English-speaking man (or subsystem) has. Indeed, in the case as described, the Chinese subsystem is simply a part of the English subsystem, a part that engages in meaningless symbol manipulation according to rules in English.[5]

But against Searle is the argument that the individual neurons in human brains also blindly follow rules and fire unconsciously, so saying that a digital computer cannot be conscious would seemingly commit one to saying that a human brain cannot be either for the same reason. Searle (1998) argues against this by saying:

> Several things are wrong with this analogy, but the most important is this: the crucial difference between the neurons and the symbols in computers is that the neurons act *causally* to cause consciousness and other mental phenomena by specific biological mechanisms. But the zeroes and ones are purely abstract. Their only causal power is the power of the implementing medium, the hardware, to produce the next stage of the program when the machine is running.[6]

For the Chinese Room argument to work, it is required that human brains work in a fundamentally different way to digital computers. But this causal power of brains is not something that Searle claims to know anything about. You could argue virtually anything about the brain until we know everything about it. It seems that the onus is on Searle to demonstrate his claim that the brain is fundamentally different to a digital computer, but before committing to a viewpoint let's first see what he says about intentionality.

Intentionality

Along similar lines to the Chinese Room is the digital computer that functions exactly like a human brain. In this computer, each neuron is replaced by a functionally equivalent silicon chip. The Chinese

---

[5] pp. 359–360
[6] p. 59, italics in original

Room might be more believable as it is not specified that it can have conversations at anywhere near human level. It might be like one of today's attempts at passing the Turing Test. So in this sense the human brain simulator is a step up and you might need more convincing of its logical possibility.

It is based on the possibility of at least weak artificial intelligence (AI). Weak AI (Searle's own term) is when a computer can replicate humans' functioning exactly but without consciousness. Strong AI is when both responses and consciousness are replicated. Some would argue that even weak AI is impossible in principle (see my discussion of Roger Penrose's views, to come next in this chapter). However, neurons themselves are generally considered to be relatively simple firing devices; it is just the arrangement that is complex. If a neuron can be functionally replicated, and I see no reason why not (e.g. Chalmers (1996, p. 254) says they could work using look-up tables), then in principle so can the arrangement of neurons. There is some debate as to how complex an individual neuron is, but it would require more than complexity to stop them from being reproduced digitally in principle. It would require there to be a more fundamental problem, and there is a lack of evidence that this problem exists. This clears the way for at least a discussion about a silicon-chip brain that replicates human responses exactly.

John Searle (e.g. 1998, pp. 146–147) believes that such a brain is not necessarily beyond the realms of possibility, but that the brain would not be conscious. Searle does not believe that functioning is the important factor in consciousness, which is clear from what we've already seen of his views. He thinks the important factor is intentionality.

The philosophical term 'intentionality' has nothing to do with intentions. Intentionality is basically 'aboutness'. When people talk about the intentional states of something, they are talking about what it is about, or what it 'points to' in the real world. For example, if you draw a picture of a horse, it is supposed to be about a horse, so it has horse intentionality.

According to Searle (e.g. 1992), the difference between computers and us is the nature of our intentionality. Our brains have intrinsic intentionality and computers have derived, or as-if (i.e. not real), intentionality. Our brain states do not need to be interpreted by anyone for them to have meaning or aboutness – they are observer-independent. Computer programs are, according to Searle, observer-relative, since the meaning only comes from the application.

I'll start with a simple example of derived intentionality. Imagine a calculator that just has the four basic operators of add, subtract, multiply and divide, and the digits 0 to 9. Somebody who has never seen a calculator before, and doesn't know how to read any mathematical symbols, could come along and interpret the calculator in a different way to everyone else. This person might decide that 1 on the calculator means 'two', 2 means 'four', with every number taking on double its intended value. When he tried to do certain calculations, he would conclude that the + and – symbols do actually mean plus and minus. However, the x and / symbols would not translate as smoothly. For us, the calculation '7 x 8 = 56' would mean quite simply 'seven times eight equals fifty-six'. But for our chap, it would mean 'fourteen x sixteen equals one hundred and twelve'. Multiplication would not fit here since fourteen times sixteen equals two hundred and twenty-four. The operator 'x' would actually mean half of the product of the two numbers. Likewise, the division sign would not mean division. If he typed in '9 / 3', he would get 3. So this would mean 'eighteen / six equals six'. The symbol that is division for us would for him mean double the quotient of the two numbers.

What this person has done is find a consistent way of interpreting the output of a calculator that is different from the standard interpretation. It could be argued that the standard interpretation is the correct one because that is how it was intended to be used. But there is nothing intrinsic to the calculator itself that makes one interpretation more correct than any other. This is what Searle means when he says that digital computers lack intrinsic intentionality. As far as the calculator is concerned there is no right or wrong interpretation. Its intentionality is not real, according to Searle, but it is given as-if intentionality by the designers or operators. According to Searle, this is the difference between humans and digital computers. It is our intrinsic intentionality, says Searle, that gives us real understanding and real consciousness.

Searle's argument is that the silicon-chip brain is not conscious despite its equivalent complexity to a human brain, because its processing would be observer-relative, and could be interpreted in another way. But unfortunately Searle gives no explanation of how or why human brains have intrinsic intentionality in contrast to digital computers, and gives no mechanism by which intrinsic intentionality could even exist. There is no explanation of what makes brains special.

The one argument seems to be that we know how computers work and that they are obviously not conscious, whereas we do not know how human brains work but they obviously are conscious. That seems to be on very shaky ground, particularly as it seems quite clear that human consciousness would have to result in some way from the blind firing of neurons, which does not, on the face of it, seem to be a more plausible consciousness-creator than the blind manipulation of symbols in computers as it suffers from the same basic problem. So Searle's argument is left in the same position as it was before we discussed intentionality.

Dennett (e.g. 1996a, pp. 50–55) does not believe that there is such a thing as intrinsic intentionality. A sentence or a calculator only has meaning in the context in which it exists and so, according to Dennett, do brains. A man-made artefact gets its intentionality from the person who made it, and, according to Dennett, human brains get their intentionality from their creator: evolution by natural selection, which is itself blind. There is no obvious reason to conclude that brains' intentionality is any more real than any other intentionality, further casting doubt on the concept of intrinsic intentionality.

Brains are subject to the same blind laws of physics as all other objects, and if they can be conscious then there is no reason to discount the possibility that digital computers can be conscious too. Searle is arguing from our ignorance of how human brains work, so I think his argument has a sell-by date.

Block (1978) argues against functionalism by saying that it would be possible to get every person in China to simulate the behaviour of a neuron. They could communicate neural firings by radio link and control an artificial body. Alternatively, Block suggests that each neuron could be represented by a beer can in a similar way. Intuitively these systems may not seem like they should be conscious. But, as with the Chinese Room, that does not count as proof that they are not. Chalmers (1996) argues that it is equally implausible that the brain, which is just a 'hunk of gray matter' (p. 251), should be conscious. Searle (1998, p. 158) argues that we know from first-hand experience that the brain does produce consciousness. However, this does not refute the idea that the Chinese Nation or beer can systems are also conscious, however counterintuitive that idea may be. So functionalism is left untouched by these arguments. I will leave it there for now until I have developed the ground in other areas, but as you can probably see, functionalism is fast emerging as a realistic candidate.

Penrose, Gödel, and Quantum Physics

British mathematician and physicist turned philosopher Roger Penrose (e.g. 1989, 1994, 1996) is of the view that even weak AI is impossible in principle, and that human brains cannot be simulated by digital computers. He is not against functionalism as such, but claims that digital computers would be irrelevant to the functionalism debate, since they cannot perform the same functions as a human brain. Like Searle, he argues that brains have special properties, but on the details they disagree.

Penrose argues that human thought is not computable on a digital computer because it involves non-algorithmic quantum processes. The main thrust of his argument is based on Kurt Gödel's incompleteness theorem. From Penrose (1994):

> Among the things that Gödel indisputably established was that no *formal system* of sound mathematical rules of proof can ever suffice, even in principle to establish all the true propositions of ordinary arithmetic.[7]

Statements that are true but cannot be proved within a given system are known as 'Gödel sentences'. Although they are mathematical statements, they can be shown to be equivalent to an assertion that

---

[7]   pp. 64–65, italics in original

they cannot be proved within the system. To take an example from Searle (1998):

17. Statement number 17 is not provable in this system.[8]

Penrose attempts to use this as a proof that human thought is not algorithmic. Any digital computer would have its own Gödel sentences that are true but that it would not be able to prove (see Penrose, 1994, pp. 72–76). We humans, however, would be able to see that the statements are true using our insight, and therefore are not like digital computers, according to Penrose.

Penrose's reasoning is very mathematical and sometimes quite obscure, but I do not think I need to go into the precise mathematical detail of it here for you to understand the gist of it. I would only be repeating what Penrose has said anyway, so if you want to find out more, it's probably best just to get it straight from the horse's mouth.

Let's assume for the sake of argument that human thought can be represented on a digital computer. What sort of computational system might be able to represent human thought? Not one restricted to the mind of one human. After all, Penrose states that it would be within the scope of our algorithm to refer to 'the reasoning and insights of "mathematicians" or "the mathematical community"' (1994, p. 97). So we can look at this as a collective human-thought algorithm rather than a specific person's algorithm.

We have available to us more than our thoughts in our heads to find mathematical truths. It goes much further than this. We use various resources, including paper to work on, calculators, and computers. We can consult each other and we can delve deeper and deeper into the world and universe to find resources to help us prove mathematical theorems. So the algorithm in question could involve the workings of a sizeable part of the universe, which we are assuming for the time being to be computable.

If human thought is algorithmic in this way, then there must be a Gödel sentence (in fact an infinite number of them) that is true, but that we cannot know is true. Penrose argues that no such Gödel sentence could stump us in this way, showing that our thinking

---

[8]   p. 64

cannot be algorithmic. This is because, as discussed above, when we came across this Gödel sentence, we would be able to just see that it was true. The argument certainly has an amount of intuitive appeal. Faced with our own Gödel sentence, surely we would be able to see its truth, using plain common sense, since it would have to be true by the mere fact that it is a Gödel sentence. After all, who wouldn't be able to see that statement 17 was true? This would then create a contradiction, since it is only our Gödel sentence on the basis that we can't prove it to be true. This contradiction then nullifies the premise that our thought is algorithmic and that we can have a Gödel sentence. This is the basis of Penrose's argument.

But Penrose's argument does not succeed unless we can actually find out the algorithmic procedure involved, which we need to do in order to find the Gödel sentence itself. If you found mathematical truths using some algorithmic procedure, it would be no contradiction for you to follow through Penrose's reasoning, and say that there must be a specific true statement that is unknowable to you because of your algorithmic procedure. The contradiction would only occur if you could find a specific Gödel sentence in its mathematical form and prove it to be so, and therefore see that it is true. Unless Penrose can show that this could happen under the assumption that our mathematical reasoning is algorithmic, his argument fails. This is quite clear because it would be easy to program a digital computer to draw the conclusion that it has a Gödel sentence, and that this sentence must be true, without stating what the sentence in its mathematical form actually is. We would not see that as a contradiction. It would also be no good if someone simply told us our Gödel sentence, because this is not the same as proving that it is our Gödel sentence. And as before, a digital computer could be put in exactly the same position.

So can we find our algorithm? Quite simply, no. When we look at what is involved in our own algorithmic procedure, we can quite clearly see that there is no way that we could possibly find it, even if we did exclude some (or even virtually all) parts of the universe as inaccessible. It doesn't actually make any difference where we draw the boundary, including if we look at one brain in isolation. This is because finding the algorithm would require a system capable of containing it, but this would not be available to us. We would not have more resources for finding our mathematical algorithm than we would within the algorithm itself, but we would need to in order to be able to contain it. All the resources we have can also be used as part of our mathematical algorithm, so there is nothing else left that we can use, whether we have access to the workings of one brain or one universe. And without finding the algorithm, we would have no chance of finding its Gödel sentence (which would be incredibly complex). It seems to me that it would be impossible to do so, rather than merely very hard.

As far as I can see, Penrose's argument requires our algorithm to contain a full representation of itself. This representation would also contain a full representation and so on, leading to an infinite regress. In any case, it is up to Penrose to prove that this can be done, not for me to prove that it can't. Unless he can, his proof doesn't get off the ground.

Imagine a deterministic universe that you are outside but able to see into. Nothing you do can causally affect what is inside but you can observe everything. With the right resources, and knowledge of the workings of this universe, it would be theoretically possible for someone in this situation to calculate the positions, momentums and every other relevant detail of every particle in this universe, and so predict everything about the universe's future. For example, you could run a computer simulation of this universe that runs faster than real time. But no-one inside the universe could do this, because they would need their resources to encompass the universe and have computing power left over. The simulation inside the universe would need to contain a further copy of itself and so on ad infinitum. There is a paradoxical idea that someone could use such a simulation to predict everything that is going to happen, including their own actions, and then purposely do something else. But this paradox could never arise because no-one could ever make such a simulation or such a prediction. I see this as analogous to finding your own Gödel sentence.

The point of all this is that we simply wouldn't be able to recognise our Gödel sentence to be such, so we would not be in a position to apply our insight in the way Penrose imagines. And as before, if this can be done, then I see no reason why a digital computer could not do it. But a digital computer clearly cannot, as has been proved by Gödel. So Penrose needs to demonstrate and prove exactly what human brains can do that digital computers cannot.

Penrose also argues that mathematicians do not rely on an unconscious unknowable algorithm based at the level of neurons, but on higher-level understandable logic, and that they know and understand what they are doing (1994, p. 147). For the sake of argument, it may be the case that we can look at *some* of our reasoning in this way, but we are looking for the limits of our understanding and, for this, there is no way to avoid looking at the complex detail of our brains and outside cues. It is simply not the case that mathematicians understand exactly how all their proofs were formed, because they do not know exactly what went on in their brains when they came up with the proofs. While the resultant mathematical theorem itself would have a logical progression, many unknown factors would have been at play in helping them to put it together in the first place. The logical steps in the mathematical proof are the end result of the algorithm, not the algorithm itself.

Penrose also takes issue with the possibility that we could rely on an unconscious algorithm that was the product of natural selection to uncover mathematical truths:

> Our naturally selected putative algorithm would have to have been strong enough that, at the time of our remote ancestors, it would already have encompassed, within its potential scope, the rules of any formal system that is now considered by mathematicians to be unassailably consistent [...] The algorithm would have to have encompassed, as particular instances of itself, the potential for making precise discriminations, distinguishing valid from invalid arguments in all the, then, yet-to-be-discovered areas of mathematical activity that nowadays occupy the pages of mathematical research journals. This putative, unknowable, or incomprehensible algorithm would have to have, coded within itself, a power to do all this, yet we are being asked to believe that it arose solely by natural selection geared to the circumstances in which our remote ancestors struggled for survival.[9]

---

[9] 1994, p.149

But no-one would argue that our mathematical algorithm is purely the result of our genetic make-up and contained entirely in our brains at birth, and in the same way, a digital computer does not come already programmed with every algorithm that will be used on it. Our mathematical understanding does not all come from within, but also from our interaction with other people and the outside world, and so our algorithm would be shaped by the outside world, as I have already argued. Of course, the outside world itself was not created specifically for the solving of mathematical problems, nor did it evolve for this purpose, but it avoids Penrose's problems here because, considered as an algorithm, it is large enough and complex enough to easily contain the degrees of freedom required to enable us to do mathematics without having to be specifically designed for the purpose.

Penrose's argument is no threat to the idea that our thought is algorithmic and can be represented by a digital computer. Just as with computers, there would be true statements that humans cannot prove to be so. We would not be able to find out what these sentences were, so we would never be in a position to 'prove the unprovable', and so there is no contradiction. It is not as simple as asserting the truth of a statement that claims itself not to be provable; you need to find the mathematical statement first, and that's the hard part. We need not let Gödel's theorem bother us when postulating that human brain processes can be represented on a digital computer.

However, it would make no real difference to the ideas discussed in this book if Penrose was correct and human brains could not be represented by a digital computer. The standard silicon-chip-brain thought experiments would no longer be valid, but computers that are functionally equivalent to human brains could still be created as long as they used the same quantum principles that Penrose thinks are required. But as things stand, I will be working under the assumption that human brains can be functionally represented using silicon-chip digital computers, and these are my primary example in the discussion of functionalism.

Chapter 3

Materialism and Dualism

Is consciousness a scientific problem that we can find all the answers to by empirical studies, or are at least some parts of it beyond the reach of empirical science? This question highlights the basic difference between materialism and dualism: two categories that most positions in the discussion of consciousness fall into.

Materialism is the view that everything is physical, including any consciousness that may exist. I say 'may exist' because there are materialists who deny the existence of consciousness altogether. I will use the term 'zombic materialism' for the theory that the physical world exists without any consciousness at all. It is the view that we are all zombies. In a sense it is not a theory of consciousness, but a theory about the universe without consciousness. This view may sound ridiculous, but it is not as easy to dismiss as you might think. Sometimes the term 'eliminative materialism' is used, but if you look it up, the definitions you find are generally not explicitly against the existence of consciousness. For example, from *The Stanford Encyclopedia of Philosophy* (Ramsey, 2013):

> Eliminative materialism (or *eliminativism*) is the radical claim that our ordinary, common-sense understanding of the mind is deeply wrong and that some or all of the mental states posited by common-sense do not actually exist.[10]

And from American philosopher Paul Churchland (1981):

> Eliminative materialism is the thesis that our common-sense conception of psychological phenomena constitutes a radically false theory,

---

[10] Italics in original

a theory so fundamentally defective that both the principles and the ontology of that theory will eventually be displaced, rather than smoothly reduced, by completed neuroscience.[11]

These two definitions are certainly not stating that consciousness does not exist. And to me these definitions come across as rather vague, saying that we are wrong about consciousness but with no suggestion of what is right. You will also find the same if you search for other definitions. Zombic materialism is clear about what it is, so that is the term I will be using. Some might consider it wasteful to invent a new term, but I'd rather that than risk ambiguity. According to this theory, no conscious mental states exist. In this case there would be no such thing as phenomenal consciousness. Psychological consciousness would still exist, but it would not be truly conscious in our strict sense.

Non-zombic materialism, on the other hand, is the view that while everything is physical, consciousness does exist because consciousness itself is physical. This would mean that consciousness could be explained entirely empirically and scientifically. Within non-zombic materialism, functionalism is probably the most popular theory, or class of theories.

Dualism maintains that there is more to consciousness than just the physical, and that no number of scientific tests will yield all the answers. Dualism opposes materialism by saying that consciousness and the physical are separate types or entities. This, however, does not exclude the possibility of interaction between them. Central to dualism is that consciousness is not physical and that the laws of physics do not tell us everything about it.

So which is the more plausible position to take? This argument has been raging for years, so before presenting any sort of conclusion on it, I will have to discuss some of the arguments and thought experiments that philosophers have grappled with over the years.

I think most people would say that dualism is the more intuitively appealing of the two positions. After all, how can subjective feelings actually be physical? If they were physical, it would mean that they

---

[11] p. 67

could be measured objectively, using third-person scientific techniques. But the idea of measuring somebody else's consciousness and of learning absolutely everything about it from the outside is very counterintuitive. Conscious thoughts seem to be essentially private, whether this is actually right or not.

On the other hand, materialism does away with the need for these two separate types, so its proponents would claim that it is the simpler theory and that they have Ockham's Razor on their side. Also on the materialists' side is the apparent causal completeness of physics. This is that every physical event has a sufficient physical cause. There doesn't appear to be any need for anything non-physical, specifically a non-physical consciousness, to help explain physical events. And according to Ockham's Razor, we should not decide that something extra – something non-physical – is required without good reason.

The causal completeness of physics is something that it is hard to imagine finding evidence against. If we were to find a cause that we were previously unaware of, then for us to have noticed it, it would have had to have physical effects. We would then simply include it in our laws of physics as a physical phenomenon, as nothing in the physical effects would give us evidence to the contrary.

The 'unscientific' idea of dualism means that many scientists and philosophers do not take it seriously. But can it be dismissed so easily? Can materialism explain consciousness by itself? It seems a daunting task, but materialists often cite precedents, one of the most commonly brought up being the example of life (although not the consciousness that goes with it). It was once a common view that the process of life itself – how inanimate matter can become animate – could not be explained by physics. This view was known as 'vitalism' and the force of life was known as 'élan vital'.

But individual processes were gradually understood and life itself discovered to be just a collection of these individual processes – breathing, digestion, reproduction etc. – and so vitalism and the élan vital expired. Obviously life isn't fully understood, but it's no longer a problem at the same level that it used to be. Will consciousness go the same way, or is it a fundamentally different problem altogether? This is the question of whether the hard problem of consciousness can be solved by solving all the easy problems. In general terms, those who think there is a hard problem that exists beyond the easy problems are dualists, and those who do not are materialists.

So far, I have introduced two major divisions in the debate about consciousness: materialism versus dualism, and functionalism versus non-functionalism (I don't think there is a nice word for that). Functionalism is normally thought of as a materialist theory, but you can also have functionalist dualism. With functionalist materialism, a conscious state is simply a physical functional state, not an extra thing arising from it, whereas with functionalist dualism, a conscious state is entirely determined by a physical functional state, but not the same thing as it. Materialism and dualism can each be either functionalist or non-functionalist. These terms can probably, broadly speaking, account for most people's views on consciousness. However, as well as there being different types of dualism and materialism, not all theories can be neatly placed into one of these categories. I will now look at some of the individual theories in more detail, starting with materialist theories.

Materialism

An example of a materialist theory of consciousness is the identity theory. This says that a conscious state is the same thing as a specific physical state. It is the exact physical make-up, so the particular materials making up the physical state are important. Therefore, for the identity theorist, if two systems were functionally equivalent but made of different materials, then they would have different conscious experiences. There is an exact identity relationship between a physical state and a conscious state.

But if it is not functioning that determines consciousness, this raises the possibility that how a being functions is irrelevant to its consciousness. If this were the case, then observable behaviour (which is part of functioning) would give no indication of what its thoughts and feelings were. It could also mean that if our own conscious feelings reflected our functioning and behaviour, it would be due to pure chance as our brains just happened to be made in exactly the right way and of exactly the right material. But I do not think that the identity theory necessarily has to make quite such strong claims. Conscious experience could still be related to the functioning of the brain, but have slightly different qualities depending on the particular substance that the brain is made of, or other functionally irrelevant details. There would still be physical attributes of the two functionally equivalent brains that were the same, such as the way certain things are connected up in the same places, so the conscious experiences would not have to be completely different. Functioning would not have to be irrelevant.

What is in favour of this theory? Why say that if two brains are functionally equivalent but made of different materials, then they will have different conscious experiences? Well, if two brains have identical functional states, but are different physically, it could be said that they are only identical in some abstract sense; it is the patterns that are identical rather than the physical natures, so a functionalist theory could be seen as a sort of dualism. I will come back to the merits of this particular point shortly. But by shunning functionalism, we would be committing ourselves to a view on consciousness that does not firmly link psychological consciousness with phenomenal consciousness. It also seems that in our attempts to get the identity theory as close to functionalism as possible, we are conceding that functionalism looks like an attractive theory, but just a bit too 'dualistic'. If the only reason for going with the identity theory is that the alternative looks too much like dualism, then it hasn't got much going for it. It would be a knee-jerk reaction.

The identity theory could also be seen as a weak form of epiphenomenalism (the view that consciousness has no effect on behaviour). If two brains are functionally identical but have different conscious experiences, then it seems that at least some of the conscious thoughts must be irrelevant in determining function and behaviour, specifically the conscious thoughts dependent on the material of which the brain is made. It is, of course, possible that two different conscious experiences can have the same effects as each other and so not be epiphenomenal, but the particular flavour of them, or at least the difference between them, would be epiphenomenal. It would not be epiphenomenal in the strongest sense, since the matter that a brain is made of can make a physical difference to its surroundings. Someone might look at a brain and comment on it, for example, and would make different comments depending on what matter they found. But there would still be a weaker epiphenomenalism in that you would be unable to convey the flavour of your thoughts in anything you do, short of cracking your head open. This would, of course, be the case for any non-functionalist theory.

With the identity theory we would be left with a strange hybrid of epiphenomenalism and consciousness-potency. It seems strange that the hardware itself would have any relevance to consciousness. The implication is that the consciousness is found in the matter itself, leading to the possibility that a brick just sitting there would have its own background level of 'identity theory' consciousness, and it sounds a bit like Searle's intrinsic intentionality, discussed in chapter 2, which I rejected. Of course, we don't know what causes consciousness exactly, but the idea that the particular matter is an important factor seems unrealistic, and I will not pursue the theory any further.

So does functionalist materialism suffer because it is the view that consciousness is not identical to the physical matter itself, but rather some abstraction or pattern of it? Is this true materialism or some form of dualism? The key here is that it does not rely on anything extra to follow on from physics. As discussed already, the defining property of dualist theories is the claim that the laws of physics alone are not enough to explain consciousness. Functionalist materialism makes no such claims, so it is not dualism. Whether it succeeds in its claims is another matter, and something that will be addressed in due course.

With functionalism, not everything in the physical make-up is important for consciousness. Two brains that are not physically identical can still have the same conscious experiences, as long as all the *relevant* physical properties are the same. Consciousness is identical to a functional state rather than the whole physical make-up in materialist functionalism.

Functionalism is probably the most popular materialist theory, and it is not hard to see why. If any non-functional properties determine consciousness, you end up with an unsatisfactory weak form of epiphenomenalism, and for consciousness to be connected to our behaviour in a meaningful way, any theory would have to approach functionalism to some degree. Intuitively, anything non-functional, such as the specific nature of the hardware, should be irrelevant. So I would say at this stage that I see functionalism as the most realistic materialist theory.

Obviously I have only discussed the identity theory as an alternative here, but it is impossible to cover every possible theory that someone could come up with. But this example has highlighted the problems that any non-functionalist theory of materialism would have.

Dualism

Due to the lack of any evidence against it, I will be assuming that physics is causally complete. This presents difficulties for certain dualist theories.

To start, it means that anything affecting our behaviour would have to be physical. Only physical causes could have physical effects. So if consciousness is to have any effect on our behaviour, it would have to be physical itself. If consciousness is non-physical, as in dualistic theories, then it would have to be an impotent by-product, or epiphenomenal, and in the strongest possible sense. It would be incapable of having any physical effects whatsoever. This would mean that the intuitive belief that we are consciously controlling our actions is simply wrong. Epiphenomenalism is generally considered to be the most realistic dualistic theory, however counterintuitive it may be.

Epiphenomenalism is an example of property dualism, where consciousness is a property that arises from brain processes, as opposed to substance dualism, where there exist both physical and conscious substances. An immortal soul would be a possible example of a conscious substance. René Descartes was a substance dualist and the concept is also referred to as 'Cartesian dualism'. David Chalmers (2010, pp. 483–485) argues that if you were a brain in a vat receiving the right inputs from a computer so that you experienced a computer-simulated world rather than the 'real' physical world, then a form of substance dualism would be true in this case.

He argues that the physical world for you would be the computer-simulated world that you perceive, and that your biological brain in the non-simulated world would therefore not be part of your physical world.

> Under this hypothesis, our cognitive system involves processes quite distinct from the processes in the physical world, but there is a causal story about how they interact.[12]

However, this is not substance dualism as it is generally understood, and is not even a mind/body dualism. The dualism here is between the physics in the simulated world and the physics in the 'real' world, so it is a physics/physics dualism. The nature of the conscious mind is still open to question. If dualism were true in the normal case, and so also within the simulated world, we would have these two layers of physics as well as consciousness in the brain-in-a-vat scenario, so what we would have is a form of 'three-ism'. However, it would be a form of dualism if materialism were true in the normal case where there is no simulation or brain in a vat. Also, this conclusion depends on the perspective of the observer. One may argue that it is substance dualism from the perspective of the individual whose brain is in the vat, but this is not *the* correct perspective. It is just as valid for someone outside the vat to conclude in favour of whatever theory holds for the rest of the human population, whether that be some form of dualism, materialism, or something else. And arguably it is this wider perspective that carries more weight. In any case, this is more of a semantic side issue than a genuine philosophical point.

The view that consciousness is non-physical but still has an effect on our behaviour is known as interactionist dualism, and it doesn't have too many supporters. It may be an attractive viewpoint in that it gives our consciousness control and keeps it as non-physical and possibly more 'special', but interactionist dualism is effectively denying that the laws of physics are causally complete.

As I said earlier, if something did have a physical effect, we would simply include it as a physical phenomenon, pretty much by definition. So what would interactionist dualism actually be claiming?

---

[12] p. 483

Consciousness would have physical effects and would in that sense be measurable, so would it not just be a form of non-zombic materialism? Perhaps there is a separate consciousness-only part that cannot be measured, but then this part could reasonably be considered epiphenomenal. The part that causes behaviour would still be physical in any meaningful sense. After all, how else does one define 'physical'? As far as I can see, interactionist dualism simply has no room to exist and I will not be pursuing it. This means that dualism has already been pinned down to a theory where consciousness has no effect on our behaviour: epiphenomenalism.

David Chalmers (1996) makes a similar point about interactionist dualism.

> Imagine [...] that 'psychons' in the nonphysical mind push around physical processes in the brain, and that psychons are the seat of experience. We can tell a story about the causal relations between psychons and physical processes, and a story about the causal dynamics among psychons, without ever invoking the fact that psychons have phenomenal properties. Just as with physical processes, we can imagine subtracting the *phenomenal* properties of psychons, yielding a situation in which the causal dynamics are isomorphic. It follows that the fact that psychons are the seat of experience plays no essential role in a causal explanation, and that even in this picture experience is explanatorily irrelevant.[13]

Chalmers (2010, pp. 126–130) revisits interactionist dualism and suggests that the collapse of a waveform in quantum mechanics is arguably down to conscious observation. However, it would still require the lower-level brain processes to create this consciousness in the first place, so arguably it would be just as much these that cause the waveform collapse as the emergent consciousness. It is not a widely held view in physics that consciousness itself is important in the waveform collapse (as opposed to any form of observation, conscious or otherwise), and anything that caused the waveform collapse could still be looked at in physical terms, by considering the physical bodies of observers, and it would be no different from the examples we have already considered.

---

[13] p. 158, italics in original

Epiphenomenalism (as we will now take dualism to imply) has the same basic theories available to it as materialism. For example, one could be a functionalist epiphenomenalist or an identity theory epiphenomenalist, the only difference being that in these cases consciousness would be determined by the functional state or entire physical state rather than simply being the same thing as it. As with materialism, a non-functionalist epiphenomenal theory would involve a mismatch between the psychological and phenomenal and would have the same unsatisfactory effects.

But if consciousness is epiphenomenal, and purely an impotent by-product of brain functioning, then how do we know about it? It would have no effect on how we function and behave. All of our beliefs would be formed by the physical brain with no reference to consciousness. So why would we believe that we are conscious?

Why people should believe in and talk about their own consciousness if it is epiphenomenal is known as the Paradox of Phenomenal Judgement (see Chalmers, 1996, pp. 172–209). There are people who say that this works strongly against epiphenomenalism, or even refutes it outright. There is a psychological belief in phenomenal consciousness, but the psychological would have no access to the phenomenal, so we would seemingly have no reason to form this belief.

However, the Paradox of Phenomenal Judgement is just as much a problem for zombic materialists, who deny the existence of consciousness altogether, as it is for epiphenomenalists. The problem of why physical beings should talk about consciousness when it is epiphenomenal is exactly the same as the problem of why physical beings should talk about consciousness when it does not exist. In both cases physical beings are talking about something that they have no access to. The fact that it happens to exist in one of the cases is irrelevant. We are looking at why a certain behaviour (talk of consciousness) would exist in two physically identical situations, while assuming that the physical is the only cause of behaviour. It may be a counterintuitive situation, but this alone does not make it fatal to either epiphenomenalism or zombic materialism.

Zombies are in their element in discussions about epiphenomenalism, and you won't have to travel far to find talk of zombies when reading about the subject. I will use them as a tool here to discuss the Paradox of Phenomenal Judgement. According to American philosopher Todd Moody (1994), zombie cultures would never develop talk of consciousness, and they wouldn't understand what we were talking about if we visited their planet and told them of this mysterious result of brain activity. (He talks about zombies in the looser sense of non-conscious beings, rather than ones that are functionally equivalent to humans.) According to Moody, they would make no sense of the Other Minds Problem. However, an individual zombie brought up in our world may go unnoticed:

> But I hope that I have shown that while it is true that zombies who grew up in our midst might become glib in the use of our language, including our philosophical talk about consciousness and dreams, a world of zombies could not *originate* these exact concepts as they are played out in philosophical discourse and imaginative idea-play, such as science fiction.[14]

The problem of whether zombies are logically possible is different from whether, in a world of non-conscious beings, they would in fact be true zombies (functionally equivalent to humans). Moody seems to be suggesting that they are logically possible (such as in the case where they are brought up among us), but that such non-conscious beings would not be true zombies if left to their own devices.

Imagine an alien world where the life on it has evolved to the point where it is advanced enough to have developed language. Some human scientists visit this world in the belief that only humans are conscious and that all the aliens on this planet are non-conscious. They also learn the language.

They observe an alien tripping over and injuring itself. One of the scientists interviews the alien and says (translated back into English), 'I don't suppose you really mind about falling over because, being non-conscious, you don't feel anything.' What would the alien say in response? Would it agree with the scientist? Imagine if it said, 'You're right. I have no feelings so I don't really mind what happens

---

[14] p. 199, italics in original

to me.' Is that likely? Clearly not. Evolution dictates that self-preservation would be at the centre of its behaviour, regardless of whether it actually is conscious. It would therefore have to insist that what happens does matter. And it would not be enough to say that it mattered 'just because'. It would have to be able to justify it, at least to itself, and presumably it would be able to put this into words. Otherwise it might be possible to convince it that its self-preservation was not worthwhile. It would also not be plausible for it to say, 'I have no feelings, but the fall registered in my brain as something which is to be avoided in terms of maximising my potential survival and reproduction.' This sort of reasoning would clearly never evolve as it is far too convoluted and would not be very convincing – for the alien or anyone else.

The simplest and most plausible mechanism for self-preservation is for the alien to say that it hurt, as well as to have similar withdrawal mechanisms to painful stimuli as we do. If it could be convinced that the pain was not real, it would damage its survival chances. It would therefore insist that it felt pain – real pain that really hurt.

So the scientist then says, 'But you're not actually conscious, are you? And you have no reason to philosophise about something you don't have. So I take it your philosophers don't talk about the problem of consciousness.' What would the alien say to this? Would it say, 'You're right. I have feelings but they're not conscious feelings. We don't philosophise about consciousness'? No, it is more likely that it would say, 'All consciousness is is to have inner feelings. I have feelings of pain among other things, so of course I'm conscious. And of course we have philosophers who are trying to work out how something like subjective feelings can possibly arise from physical matter.' After all, if, when pressed, it admitted that it wasn't really conscious, its self-preservation might suffer as a result. Things have to seem important to these aliens, from an evolutionary point of view. I actually find the concept of Moody's 'zombies' – beings with language claiming not to be conscious – a rather bizarre idea. They would not evolve.

Are the aliens described here any different from us? The aliens claim to be conscious because evolution has dictated that they do.

Whether they actually are conscious is a separate issue. The same could be said of us. But the point is that even if physical functioning only resulted in an epiphenomenal consciousness or did not result in consciousness at all, the psychological belief in consciousness would still evolve.

Obviously this is a very brief explanation and it could still be that a belief in one's own consciousness could only evolve alongside the existence of a potent consciousness for other reasons. However, going by the causal completeness of physics, it has to be possible for a belief in consciousness to evolve purely as a result of physical processing. It is a separate argument to say that this would have to involve the existence of consciousness as a potent force, and the Paradox of Phenomenal Judgement is not this argument. Further arguments would be required. The Paradox of Phenomenal Judgement works on our intuitions but, as an argument against epiphenomenalism, does not hold up to scrutiny.

A being with an epiphenomenal consciousness would be under the impression that consciousness was causing its actions, but would be wrong. But since the consciousness is simply a by-product of the processing, the psychological thoughts and phenomenal thoughts could still match perfectly, so the epiphenomenal consciousness would still think it was in control. This is why consciousness does not have to seem epiphenomenal even if it is.

But then how could an impotent by-product ever evolve? Well, quite simply, it would not evolve in its own right. It would simply be a by-product (an impotent one) of something that did! Psychological consciousness would evolve with phenomenal consciousness in tow.

At this point, it is worth bringing up again Raymond Smullyan's argument against epiphenomenalism from his story, 'An Unfortunate Dualist', mentioned in chapter 1. If there is an epiphenomenal consciousness resulting from brain activity, it could well be that there is a logical connection that cannot simply be removed. So just because it seems plausible under an epiphenomenal view that one could simply remove the consciousness with a drug and leave the functioning intact, it does not mean that it would actually be possible.

The Paradox of Phenomenal Judgement is not the biggest problem for epiphenomenalism, however. Even if we understood why people in general believe in consciousness, we would have a separate problem in finding a scientific or logical reason to believe in something that has no effects.

Daniel Dennett (1991) argues that believing in an epiphenomenal consciousness is not a serious view and likens it to a belief in epiphenomenal gremlins:

> Consider, for instance, the hypothesis that there are fourteen epiphenomenal gremlins in each cylinder of an internal combustion engine. These gremlins have no mass, no energy, no physical properties; they do not make the engine run smoother or rougher, faster or slower. There is *and could be* no empirical evidence of their presence, and no empirical way in principle of distinguishing this hypothesis from its rivals: there are twelve or thirteen or fifteen ... gremlins. By what principle does one defend one's wholesale dismissal of such nonsense?[15]

Indeed, there could be no empirical reason for believing in the gremlins, as there would be no measurable effects, and the same would apply for an epiphenomenal consciousness. The point is that we cannot reasonably state that we are conscious unless consciousness is having an effect on what we are saying. As said, there is the possibility that we could logically deduce that consciousness results from brain activity, but this has not been done yet, so for now I will just be considering empirical evidence. The empirical evidence would always be the same in the case of epiphenomenalism as in the case of zombic materialism: i.e. there would be none in favour of consciousness. So if we are taking physics seriously (which we are), then consciousness would need to be physical for us to reason that it exists. If the brain's physical reasoning processes cause it to reach the conclusion that it is conscious when consciousness is an impotent by-product, then the reasoning has to be flawed.

---

[15] pp. 403–404, ellipsis and italics in original

Mary the Colour Scientist – a Comeback for Dualism?

I will now consider a widely discussed thought experiment in the philosophy of consciousness: the Knowledge Argument and the case of Mary the Colour Scientist devised by Australian philosopher Frank Jackson (1982, 1986). This is an argument for dualism.

Mary is a scientist who has spent her whole life in a black and white room, and everything she has ever seen has been black and white. She has never seen anything of any other colour. But she also knows everything about the neurophysiology of vision and what happens in the human brain when it sees coloured objects. So what happens when Mary finally leaves her black and white room and sees a coloured object, say, red? According to Jackson, she will not have previously known what it is like to see a red object, so she will learn something new, despite already knowing all the relevant physical facts. This, according to Jackson, means that conscious experiences are not covered by physical facts, therefore materialism is false.

But does this argument really work against materialism? Dennett (1991) argues not. According to Dennett, if Mary truly knew absolutely everything physical (rather than just a lot), then she would be able to work out what it would look like to see red:

> And she knows precisely which effects – in neurophysiological terms – each particular color will have on her nervous system. So the only task that remains is for her to figure out a way of identifying those neurophysiological effects "from the inside." You may find you can readily imagine her making a *little* progress on this – for instance, figuring out tricky ways in which she would be able to tell that some color, whatever it is, is *not* yellow or *not* red. How? By noting some salient and specific reaction that her brain would have only for yellow and only for red. But if you allow her even a little entry into her color space in this way, you should conclude that she can leverage her way to complete advance knowledge, because she doesn't just know the *salient* reactions, she knows them all.[16]

Dennett continues the thought experiment in his own way: when Mary is released, she is shown a blue banana but knows it is a trick

---

[16]   pp. 400–401, italics in original

because she already knows what effect a blue or yellow object would have on her nervous system and on her thoughts. Dennett (e.g. 2005) continues his line of thought in other work.

However, it is still possible that she would not know in advance what yellow or blue actually looked like but be able to work out what colour the banana is. She might work out the colour by subtle changes in her mood, for example, but still learn what the colour actually looks like when she sees the banana.

But of course, she may go better and be able to imagine a coloured object, and so already know what it looks like, rather than merely be able to identify the colour on sight. To continue on from Dennett, perhaps she could do this by using a feedback method – looking at readout of her brain function and trying various things with her mind to get it to match up with predicted readout from seeing that colour, perhaps in the same way that some people try to learn how to slow their pulse rate.

It's *possible* that she would be able to do all this, but that's not really the point. Finding a way of imagining colours from the inside like this would be doing something extra with her complete physical knowledge. She could still have complete physical knowledge but not even attempt to learn anything more. From Jackson (1986):

> The contention about Mary is not that, despite her fantastic grasp of neurophysiology and everything else physical, she *could not imagine* what it is like to sense red; it is that, as a matter of fact, she *would not know*. But if physicalism is true, she would know; and no great powers of imagination would be called for. Imagination is a faculty that those who *lack* knowledge need to fall back on.[17]

We are concerned with the mere possibility of knowing all the relevant physical facts and not knowing what it is like to see colour. The possibility of already knowing what it is like is irrelevant; Dennett's argument would require the impossibility of not knowing. So far, the materialists still have a case to answer.

Let's say for the sake of argument that it is possible for Mary to know everything physical but still learn something new when she

---

[17] p. 291, italics in original; 'physicalism' can be seen as a synonym for 'materialism'

sees colours for the first time. She will go into the outside world and declare that she has seen colours for the first time, and has finally learnt what it is like.

Is this a refutation of materialism? For all types of materialism? If this is the case then it is also a refutation of zombic materialism. It is also worth noting that the new knowledge Mary gains when she enters the outside world would not be epiphenomenal knowledge. The point is that she would go out of the room, see a red object, and tell everyone that she has learnt what it is like to see red. Epiphenomenalism is the same as zombic materialism apart from the fact that with epiphenomenalism, consciousness is created as an impotent – and irrelevant to this case – by-product. It can have no effect on our behaviour. Mary's behaviour on leaving the room would be identical under these two views because, physically, they are the same as each other. If Mary's announcement upon leaving the room is enough to refute materialism, then it also refutes epiphenomenalism. This effectively leaves interactionist dualism, so Jackson's thought experiment would effectively prove that physics is not causally complete. This would immediately cause us a headache given what I have already said on this matter. Jackson's first (1982) paper on the subject is actually called *Epiphenomenal Qualia* and is a defence of epiphenomenalism, so it seems that he didn't realise the full ramifications of his own argument.

Has something gone wrong somewhere? It would appear that Mary's brain cannot be entirely governed by the laws of physics. But this seems to be a very strong, and strange, claim. It seems to prove too much. So let's go back. Does the Knowledge Argument really refute all kinds of materialism?

Mary's brain is a physical system (or so we will assume for now). And from a materialistic viewpoint, it is simply neural arrangements that cause people to talk about having certain experiences and feelings. Due to the make-up of her brain, Mary can answer any question about the neurophysiology of vision, and prior to leaving her room she would be able to explain to you exactly what would happen in her brain if she were to see red. She would also be able to tell you what her reactions would be. But when she actually sees red for the first time, it is also the first time that her brain has actually found itself in the particular arrangement for seeing red, and so it is the first time that she actually has those reactions. So she may well say that she is having the experience for the first time, and that she didn't previously know what it was like. Even from a materialistic point of view, having a full understanding of the neurophysiology of seeing red is different from having your brain in the correct state for seeing red. A non-physical consciousness (or indeed any type of consciousness) does not actually have to exist for this to happen; you can just see it as a physically programmed response to a novel situation.

Mary's full understanding of the neurophysiology of vision is also unlikely to be an all-at-once understanding. She could work out step by step the states her brain would pass through upon seeing red, but would at no point have the entire picture in her brain at one time. Perhaps if she could do this, she would gain an understanding equivalent to actually seeing red, but this is likely to require her brain to contain a full representation of itself resulting in an infinite regress. This is not something we need to worry about.

This situation has been compared to the difference between 'knowledge how' and 'knowledge that' (see Churchland, 1989, for a fuller discussion of this). You can know everything physical but not know how to do everything, such as ride a bike. On an intellectual level you would know what your body would have to do (knowledge that), but that is not the same as physically being able to do it (knowledge how). Similarly, Mary would know how her neurons would need to be arranged for her to experience red (knowledge that), but this is not the same as being able to put her mind in the 'seeing red' state and therefore know what it looks like (knowledge how). And I think it's reasonable to say that you can have a complete physical knowledge without having all forms of knowledge how.

However, if this still seems unsatisfactory, and you think that Mary should still be able to imagine red if she has all physical knowledge, then this is still not such a problem for materialism. You could simply say that for Mary to know everything physical, she would need to know how to put her brain in the 'seeing red' state. This is still a purely physical state of affairs and nothing non-physical needs to be postulated at any stage. So instead of saying that prior to leaving her room Mary knew everything physical but lacked knowledge, we would simply say that at that stage, Mary did not know everything physical. It simply means that we would be making more stringent requirements on what it means to know everything physical.

Personally, I would say that the ability to put her brain into a certain state would not count as physical knowledge. If you included that, you would have to include any ability whatsoever, and I think that would be inappropriate. But philosophically it doesn't matter either way.

Nothing here requires dualism to be the case. The case of Mary the Colour Scientist is not sufficient to disprove the causal completeness of physics and not enough to disprove materialism. It is now time to move on.

A Way to Avoid Materialism and Dualism?

So far, non-zombic materialists appear to have the advantage over the dualists. Consciousness, according to these materialists, is physical and can be measured empirically and objectively, unlike an epiphenomenal consciousness. This is obviously a negative for epiphenomenalism, but it is not a knockdown argument, as epiphenomenalism has not been proved false. It has already been made clear, pretty much by definition, that in dualism, consciousness is beyond measurable science. What we have seen is just another way of putting it. In any case, we have not ruled out the possibility of finding some logical connection between brains and consciousness, which does not require empirical evidence to prove. However, clinging onto the possibility of future evidence where none currently exists is, generally speaking, not a good idea.

As discussed earlier, not every theory linking consciousness and brains falls directly into dualism or materialism. Materialism is a form of monism, which means there is only one type, as opposed to two in dualism. But materialism is not the only form of monism. Monism can be neutral with regards to the physical and consciousness, so instead of saying that consciousness is physical, it could say that both consciousness and the physical have equal billing and are of the same basic type. Alternatively, there is consciousness monism. The idea that everything is consciousness or ideas is known as 'idealism'. It could be, for example, that there is no matter at all, and it is all an illusion coming from your consciousness. This view has been attributed to eighteenth-century philosopher Bishop George Berkeley. Idealism certainly cannot be simply refuted, and I will come back to it in the final chapter, but at the moment I am assuming physics as a starting point. Since idealism does away with physics, it is a non-starter under this assumption.

Chalmers (1996) discusses the idea of how physical particles could be intrinsically phenomenal or protophenomenal in nature. By 'protophenomenal' he means that the individual particles would not be conscious themselves but the combinations of several of them would be.

> There is only one class of intrinsic, nonrelational property with which we have any direct familiarity, and that it the class of phenomenal properties. It is natural to speculate that there may be some relation or even overlap between the uncharacterized intrinsic properties of physical entities, and the familiar intrinsic properties of experience. Perhaps, as [Bertrand] Russell suggested, at least some of the intrinsic properties of the physical are themselves a variety of phenomenal property? The idea sounds wild at first, but on reflection it becomes less so. After all, we really have *no idea* about the intrinsic properties of the physical. Their nature is up for grabs, and phenomenal properties seem as likely a candidate as any other.[18]

Chalmers suggests that this theory could be seen as a form of monism, and that if the intrinsic properties are phenomenal it could be idealism, whereas if they are merely protophenomenal then it could be a neutral monism.

But these intrinsically conscious particles have problems. Such particles would presumably not have any idea of the overall picture, in the same way that individual particles in a system generally don't, so I cannot see how in this case the consciousness would relate to

---

[18] pp. 153–154, italics in original

what is happening in a human brain at a higher structural level rather than being a lump of untamed consciousness or many individual consciousnesses. Daniel Dennett (2005, pp. 11–12) makes a similar point, saying that if cells themselves had a tiny bit of consciousness each, it would not help matters at all.

Phenomenal or protophenomenal properties within particles do not help us understand how a larger functional system, such as a brain, can have a consciousness that seems related to that functioning or higher-level organisation. The fact that the individual particles might have a consciousness of their own seems irrelevant here. If they do, then it seems that we must actually have two different types of consciousness at once: the consciousness we normally think of and this sum of the tiny consciousnesses of each particle. These particles also sound a lot like the psychons of interactionist dualism, which Chalmers did not have much time for.

To be fair, Chalmers only suggested this idea to show that epiphenomenalism is not necessarily the only solution, although he revisits the idea in his later book (2010, pp. 133–137). I do not think that it is a workable idea.

Generally speaking, the idea of a neutral monism seems a bit vague and a case of wanting to have your cake and eat it. If we are assuming that physics is purely physical, then this has to be the end of the road for that type of theory. When I lift the physical assumption in the final chapter, I will cover some of these ideas in a different light, however.

John Searle (e.g. 1998) has his own way of avoiding both materialism and dualism. He does not think that dividing consciousness and matter into two categories is the right way of looking at it, and takes what he seems to see as a common-sense approach. Searle argues that consciousness is not some extra ingredient, but is a biological phenomenon like any other. He calls his view 'biological naturalism' (p. xiv). Searle does not claim to be a materialist because he doesn't think that consciousness is actually a physical thing or process. He doesn't claim to be a dualist because he believes that consciousness is no different from other biological processes.

> In my view we have to abandon dualism and start with the assumption that consciousness is an ordinary biological phenomenon comparable with growth, digestion, or the secretion of bile.[19]

Is this a reasonable view? If Searle sees consciousness as just another biological process, wouldn't this just be materialism? Apparently not, because, as said, Searle believes that consciousness isn't equivalent to any physical process. But the other biological processes (e.g. digestion) are purely physical, so consciousness is still marked out as different, seemingly now making it dualism.

Searle's position is a tricky one to maintain. He wants to avoid materialism since he does not believe that consciousness is a physical process itself; he recognises it as a first-person phenomenon that can't be reduced to a third-person phenomenon. He also wants to avoid dualism because he thinks consciousness is potent (i.e. not epiphenomenal), and presumably does not want to deny the causal completeness of the physical, which means he cannot embrace interactionist dualism.

Searle does not deny the logical possibility of beings that are functionally equivalent to us but are not conscious, as I have already discussed in chapter 2. If functionally equivalent beings with silicon-chip brains were made, they would be such beings, according to Searle. If these zombies are a possibility, then it may lead some people to conclude that consciousness is epiphenomenal. After all, what does consciousness do if these zombies can exist? But, as said, Searle is not an epiphenomenalist, and believes that our consciousness causes our behaviour:

> I hit my thumb with a hammer. This causes me to feel a conscious, unpleasant sensation of pain. My pain in turn causes me to yell "Ouch!"[20]

So if we hit ourselves with a hammer, then it is the conscious pain that causes us to say 'Ouch', whereas if the zombie with the silicon-chip brain hit itself, it would instead say 'Ouch' because of some non-conscious functional state. But it is not simply a case of humans

---

[19] p. 6
[20] p. 148

and zombies being the same apart from consciousness existing in humans. It would also appear that zombies have something that humans do not. If it is consciousness that causes us to shout out, and zombies do not have consciousness, then they must have something extra to compensate for their lack of consciousness that causes their exclamation. This is unless humans actually have both systems (consciousness and the zombie functional state), which both have exactly the same effects and therefore never interfere with each other. This situation is known as causal overdetermination and is an extreme violation of Ockham's Razor, and very implausible. It is not clear what the zombies could have that humans do not, particularly if they are designed to be functionally equivalent.

Chalmers (1996, p. 152) also discusses causal overdetermination as a possible way of avoiding epiphenomenalism, where the physical is causally complete and also a non-physical consciousness controls our behaviour, but in exactly the same way with no conflict: a bit like two people pushing a trolley of neglible mass up a hill at a constant speed so that if one lets go, it carries on as if nothing has happened. However, as discussed with Searle's theory, this is a very unrealistic theory, and not one I would pursue.

Unless physics is causally incomplete (and I doubt Searle would say it is), all of human behaviour can be explained in physical terms. Since we have discarded causal overdetermination, this leaves Searle's theory with no room left.

In the run up to the next chapter, I think it is worth saying that while Searle is not a functionalist, he would presumably still say that in cases where there is intrinsic intentionality and, therefore, consciousness, the consciousness is in some way related to functioning, or there would be no way of correlating consciousness with action, in the same way as we discussed with the identity theory. Since Searle obviously sees these as related, he would be in some sense an intrinsic intentionality functionalist. This means that while functional architecture alone would not result in a conscious state, where there is intrinsic intentionality, that intentionality would work its magic on the functional architecture or at least something close, so that the way we think and the way we act correlate with each other: a match between phenomenal and psychological. However, his views on what might happen if someone's neurons were replaced one by one with functionally equivalent silicon chips are revealing:

> A second possibility, also not to be excluded on any a priori grounds, is this: as the silicon is progressively implanted into your dwindling brain, you find that the area of your conscious experience is shrinking, but that this shows no effect on your external behaviour. You find to your total amazement, that you are indeed losing control of your external behaviour. You find, for example, that when the doctors test your vision, you hear them say, "We are holding up a red object in front of you; please tell us what you see." You want to cry out, "I can't see anything. I'm going totally blind." But you hear your voice saying in a way that is completely out of your control, "I see a red object in front of me." If we carry this thought experiment to the limit, we get a much more depressing result than last time. We imagine that your conscious experience slowly shrinks to nothing, while your externally observable behavior remains the same.[21]

Chalmers (1996) quotes the same passage and points out that there is simply no room in the brain for these thoughts to occur.

> There is no room for it in the neurons, which after all are identical to a subset of the neurons supporting the usual beliefs; and Searle is surely not suggesting that the silicon replacement is itself supporting the new beliefs![22]

But this is not my main point in bringing up the passage. It seems that, according to Searle, where intrinsic intentionality (and therefore consciousness) is present, the consciousness that does arise does not have to reflect the functioning. It seems that the two are, at least to a degree, independent. This means that in beings whose consciousness relates to their functioning, it is only by the chance correlation between intrinsic intentionality and functioning in their particular case.

Searle only suggested this scenario as one possibility of what could happen, and a belief in intrinsic intentionality does not commit one to the outcome outlined above. However, it does seem

---

[21]   1992, pp. 66–67
[22]   p. 258

anyway that intrinsic intentionality is largely independent of functioning, so it seems a fairly reasonable conclusion that the two could pull in different directions, leaving thoughts and actions completely separate from each other. To me this just highlights again that intrinsic intentionality is not a realistic concept. It is also worth mentioning again that any non-functional theory of consciousness suffers from the need for a partial coincidence between consciousness and functioning. We require at least an approximation to functionalism for the consciousness to be one worth considering.

To conclude this chapter, the discussion of Searle's views, along with other theories that attempt to avoid materialism and dualism, has shown that such theories do not hold up very well in a physical universe. It is materialism versus dualism.

Chapter 4

A Conclusion on Functionalism

Here I make a conclusion that is probably one of the worst-kept secrets in this book. I felt the need to hold back the conclusion until now, so that I could discuss the other theories first.

Most theories of consciousness work on the assumption that consciousness is based on brain functioning in some way. But there are theories stating that consciousness relies on factors other than functioning, or at least in addition to functioning. For example, we've discussed the identity theory and intrinsic intentionality, but all such theories would have to be reliant on function to some extent (as discussed in chapter 3) to be coherent.

I have already concluded that any reasonable theory would have to approach functionalism, and in the absence of strong arguments to the contrary, it seems sensible now to just go the whole hog.

I cannot prove that consciousness is dependent on functional architecture, but it is the best theory available, as any other theory would be one that divorces psychological consciousness from phenomenal consciousness. We have evidence for psychological consciousness, and phenomenal consciousness is assumed to match this, or it would be just made up and not the consciousness that we are trying to find a theory on. So from this point on, I will be assuming that if consciousness results from brain activity, then it is entirely determined by the functioning of the brain. This is functionalism.

Equivalent functional architecture can be physically realised in many ways. For example in his story *A Conversation with Einstein's Brain*, Douglas Hofstadter (1981b) describes a book that contains a perfectly detailed description of Albert Einstein's brain. It can be interacted with if you follow the right procedure and modify the appropriate pages accordingly, to represent Einstein's change in brain state. It would obviously be incredibly complex, and millions of neural changes would have to be represented by this book for even the slightest of interactions, and you would have to simulate an entire realistic environment for this virtual brain to reside in and interact with. If such a book were made accurately, it would be functionally equivalent to Einstein's real brain. This book, during these interactions, should therefore be considered to have the same consciousness that Einstein would have had given the same interactions.

Chalmers (1996, see section pp. 247–275) has his own interesting arguments for functionalism based on 'fading qualia' and 'dancing qualia'. In his fading qualia thought experiment, he works under the premise that a silicon-chip brain would have no consciousness. He imagines what would happen if his neurons were replaced one by one with functionally equivalent silicon chips. His consciousness would have to either suddenly disappear at some point or gradually fade out (ignoring Searle's slightly bizarre scenario that we encountered in chapter 3). If it suddenly disappeared, there would be a seemingly arbitrary point where replacing one neuron would wipe out his consciousness altogether. He does not see this as plausible.

If consciousness fades out, then in the case where half the neurons have been replaced, Joe (as Chalmers calls this being he has become by the halfway point) would think he had a consciousness as strong as Chalmers but would simply be wrong. Chalmers finds this intermediate case less plausible than a complete zombie claiming to have conscious experiences of which it has none.

In the dancing qualia thought experiment, Chalmers considers a functional isomorph, a sort of twin, which does not lack consciousness, but simply has a different consciousness. In this example, where Chalmers sees red, his silicon isomorph sees blue. This is an example of the famous inverted spectrum, which is very popular with philosophers, and will be discussed further in chapter 6.

Since you cannot get from red to blue in ten unnoticeable steps (if you choose the right red and blue at least), there will be two brains in the series from normal brain to silicon-chip brain that differ by only 10% of their make-up but will have significantly different experiences. Chalmers then imagines having a back-up circuit created for his own brain, which replaces the relevant 10% of his neurons with silicon chips. He has a switch that he can use to flip between each system. The low figure of 10% is used, as opposed to anything higher, to avoid problems concerning personal identity and whether he is still 'the same person'.

Since the two systems are functionally equivalent, there can be nothing that represents noticing a change in experience, but as he flicks the switch back and forth, his colour experience will change in front of his eyes unnoticed by him. As with fading qualia, Chalmers does not see this as plausible. Chalmers argues:

> It would suggest once again a radical dissociation between consciousness and cognition. If this kind of thing could happen, then psychology and phenomenology would be radically out of step.[23]

This is basically the crux of the fading qualia and dancing qualia arguments. These arguments provide good illustrations of Chalmers's dislike of the possible dissociation between consciousness and cognition, and I think they work well to complement my own arguments, in order to show what is at stake if functionalism is not true. A functionalist consciousness is the most plausible one and really the only one that I am now looking for in a brain/consciousness link.

If consciousness is determined by functional architecture, then it would seem that the more complex the functional architecture, the more complex the consciousness, and the less complex the functional architecture, the less complex the consciousness. But does consciousness require a certain level of functional complexity to exist at all? I asked this in the introduction and left it open, but it has now come up again, although I am still not drawn to a strong conclusion. Since any cut-off point for consciousness seems to be arbitrary, it could be that any processing leads to some sort of consciousness, however basic. This leads us to panpsychism, the

---

[23] p. 269

view that everything is conscious. Chalmers (1996, pp. 293–301) discusses this idea and is generally positive about it, although he does not commit. From my own point of view, I will leave it as an open possibility, as I do not think it is overly important at the moment.

The main candidates that we now have for the solution to the Mind–Body Problem are functionalist materialism and functionalist epiphenomenalist dualism. So far, materialism seems to have encountered fewer problems than dualism, but this discussion is not over yet. There is still zombic materialism as well, but you could argue that it isn't really a solution to the problem, but an admission of defeat.

Chapter 5

Epiphenomenalism or Nothing

Having looked at some of the ways in which consciousness might result from brain activity, and some of the arguments people have presented, it is now time to make a clear decision on which theories hold up. Specifically, materialism and dualism (epiphenomenalism) are about to go head to head.

We have dealt with the Paradox of Phenomenal Judgement against epiphenomenalism (chapter 3), but still counting against it is Dennett's epiphenomenal gremlins argument. According to non-zombic materialists, however, consciousness is physical and can be measured empirically and objectively. This would avoid the problems of epiphenomenal gremlins.

But can consciousness be measured? We need a third-person, objective reason for believing that consciousness exists. Non-zombic materialism has been given a free ride so far in this book for making this claim, so now it's time to look at it a bit closer. If we have an advanced robot (called Prarnt) that understands the physical workings of the human brain but does not have any first-person evidence for believing in human consciousness, then what would Prarnt make of consciousness? Prarnt does not introspect and has been programmed not to consider its own thought processes (conscious or otherwise) specifically for the task. Prarnt would observe human behaviour and brain function and conclude, unsurprisingly, that everything, including our claims of being conscious, could be explained on a purely physical level. See Carter (2002, pp. 80–83) for a more lengthy discussion of how a Martian might view our brain activity and behaviour without resorting to the 'c' word.

The non-zombic materialist would not initially have a problem and would argue that consciousness is precisely the physical workings of the brain so there is still reason to believe in it. However, this is not the definition of consciousness, nor does it follow trivially from the definition, so it would have to be shown. Currently, there is no empirical evidence for the existence of phenomenal consciousness. If there were, then the materialism/dualism debate would already be over. So non-zombic materialists currently rely on the initial assumption that we are conscious. But from a scientific viewpoint, it is not enough to say that you know you are consciousness and use that as a starting point, because it cannot be proven that it is your phenomenal consciousness causing you to say that, even to yourself.

Non-zombic materialists would claim that they are in a better position than epiphenomenalists because if they are right, then their theory could at some point be shown to be correct using scientific techniques, unlike epiphenomenalism. But in terms of current evidence, their theory is just as lacking.

But Prarnt is not using only evidence that we currently have. It is a super-robot that has all the relevant physical evidence available to it. So, what third-person evidence could there be for consciousness? What would Prarnt conclude? This brings us back to whether it is possible to reduce the 'hard' problem of consciousness into its many 'easy' problems.

The problem of life was solved because it was broken down into various problems of functioning. They were big problems, but they were still in the same mould as the 'easy' problems of consciousness. So it would be wrong to say that a precedent was set here that is relevant to the hard problem of consciousness.

However, Dennett (1995) draws a comparison between consciousness and health:

> So what is health *for*? Such a mystery! But the mystery would arise only for someone who made the mistake of supposing that health was some *additional* thing that could be added or subtracted to the proper workings of all the parts. In the case of health we are not apt to make such a simple mistake, but there is a tradition of supposing just this in

the case of consciousness. Supposing that by an act of stipulative imagination you can remove consciousness while leaving all cognitive systems intact – a quite standard but entirely bogus feat of imagination – is like supposing that by an act of stipulative imagination, you can remove health while leaving all bodily functions and powers intact. If you think you can imagine this, it's only because you are confusedly imagining some health-module that might or might not be present in a body. Health isn't that sort of thing, and neither is consciousness.[24]

But health, like life, is a purely physical phenomenon and is defined in terms of bodily functioning, so cannot be divorced from it. No-one would say that there is a hard problem of health, so the comparison does not hold up. All the precedents have involved third-person physical phenomena. Consciousness is a first-person phenomenal phenomenon, so citing these precedents should not necessarily give us too much confidence when it comes to consciousness. It's not specifically that consciousness is a first-person phenomenon that is the problem, however, since arguably the psychological point of view of a zombie is a first-person point of view. It's more that it is a phenomenal problem as opposed to a strictly physical one, so it cannot necessarily be understood in third-person terms, which a zombie's point of view could be.

We can imagine what it would be like to solve the easy problems and get to the bottom of psychological consciousness. We may not have the answers now, but we do not lack the imagination to understand what the answers might look like. It would all be about how parts of the brain cause us to function in a certain way. We already have knowledge of some parts of this, and solving the problem of psychological consciousness with neuroscience would involve more understanding in this way. Obviously it would be a great increase in understanding, but it would all be of the same type: functioning and behaviour.

This is the problem. We need to cross a line where third-person evidence suddenly becomes evidence of phenomenal experience. And it would have to be a definite line. Let's not fool ourselves – currently there is zero scientific evidence for phenomenal

---

[24] p. 325, italics in original

consciousness, and any evidence at all would be *the* big break-through that would finish dualism once and for all. But with third-person evidence, we will not uncover some great magical secret of the brain that could make this breakthrough possible. Everything we learn about the brain is about functioning: exciting, yes, but more of the same as what we've already learnt.

The fact that there is doubt in some people's minds as to whether a bacterium or even a thermostat (a case where we do understand the functioning completely) has some degree of consciousness shows that this problem will not be solved by learning about the functioning of one specific object, i.e. the human brain. The problem is not simply of how human brains become conscious, but of how physical processing can in principle become conscious. Understanding the human brain will not tell us this.

By its very nature, science can only solve the easy problems: physical problems, which include functioning and behaviour. Science cannot touch the hard problem of consciousness. The only way for a materialist to escape this is to deny its existence as a problem. But the fact is that there clearly is a hard problem for all but the zombic materialists, or the discussion would be over already. You cannot make up scientific, empirical, third-person results that would give us evidence for phenomenal consciousness. Scientifi-cally, there is nowhere to start if you want to break down the hypothesis that somebody is a zombie.

Prarnt would see no reason to conclude that consciousness is the same thing as the physical functioning of the brain. Prarnt would not see any third-person evidence for consciousness, because no such evidence could exist. Prarnt would conclude against the physical existence of consciousness. Of course, materialists may argue that I am not finding consciousness here because I am looking for something 'extra', which consciousness is not. But unless you simply define consciousness to begin with in a physical or functional way, you will not find it. Non-zombic materialism can never be better than believing in epiphenomenal gremlins.

But it is worse than gremlins. If consciousness really was a third-person, physical phenomenon, as is central to non-zombic materialism, then its existence could be demonstrated using third-person techniques. This is the whole point of non-zombic material-ism, and it has failed. Non-zombic materialism is simply wrong, rather than merely unprovable. The arguments against it are fatal. Non-zombic materialists are still waiting for a big discovery in physics or neuroscience, but it is a discovery that can never and will never take place. Materialism as a scientific theory of consciousness may have had the advantage of being falsifiable (a cornerstone of scientific testability), but now it has the disadvantage of having been falsified. Saying that consciousness and the physical are one and the same was a worthwhile attempt to simplify matters, but the bottom line is that it can't be done.

Just to clarify what I'm ruling out here: as discussed in chapter 3, if physics is somehow intrinsically conscious itself, this would arguably be more of an idealism or a neutral monism, so this possi-bility (which I did not take forward anyway) is not something that would stop us from refuting a non-zombic materialism that results from purely physical physics. It is this sort of materialism that has been refuted.

We now have to conclude that there is no empirical reason for believing that phenomenal consciousness exists at all. Conscious-ness is not involved in the processing that leads us to believe we are conscious (under our basic physical assumptions from chapter 3). Consciousness would have to be epiphenomenal if it exists at all, which means that believing in any consciousness is like believing in epiphenomenal gremlins.

We also have to explicitly separate phenomenal consciousness and psychological consciousness at this stage, having previously considered that they might turn out to be one and the same. Psycho-logical consciousness, which is involved in function, and therefore existent on a physical level, is not actually conscious in our strict philosophical sense. Phenomenal consciousness is not involved in functioning, although since I concluded in favour of functionalism in the previous chapter, the two would correlate perfectly.

Where does this leave our consciousness theories? With non-zombic materialism now out of the running, this leaves us with dualistic epiphenomenalism. Epiphenomenalism still has its problems, but no new ones have been added. Prarnt sees only what is there physically, so it would not be expected to see an epiphenomenal consciousness. Prarnt has evidence against non-zombic materialism but only a lack of evidence for epiphenomenalism. The relative position of epiphenomenalism is now stronger than before. It is, in fact, the only theory of consciousness that we will take forward from here, until I question certain physical assumptions in the final chapter. Dualism is the only way to proceed from standard physical assumptions, and specifically it is functionalist epiphenomenalism that we are taking forward.

Epiphenomenalism is not the real winner here, however. Since any theory of consciousness resulting from brains is like believing in epiphenomenal gremlins, it is zombic materialism – the view that there is no phenomenal consciousness at all – that has won this battle. From a third-person scientific point of view, consciousness is not worth considering, but from a philosophical point of view, I think it still is. Since epiphenomenalism has not been disproved and remains as the only vaguely reasonable theory that keeps the consciousness/physics link alive, I think it would be interesting to keep hold of this possibility, and to explore further to see where it takes us. It is still of interest to us to see what other things follow if there is such a thing as consciousness. It would also be unsatisfactory to simply write consciousness off as non-existent at this stage, however logical or scientific it may be. It is also possible to dispute that third-person evidence takes precedence over all others. But more on that in the final chapter.

This chapter has shown that the problem of how consciousness arises from the physical is no longer a problem for science to deal with. It is a philosophical problem. But by saying that science cannot solve the problem, are we admitting defeat in some way? Since there is no direct scientific evidence for phenomenal consciousness, a hard-line scientist could say that there is no defeat; consciousness never existed as a scientific phenomenon – we only thought it did – and so there is nothing left unexplained. And in any case, we are certainly not admitting defeat unless we do not consider philosophy to be a tool for the truth. We could yet find a logical connection between physics and consciousness.

This also does not mean that science cannot help us. If we found a logical connection between physics and consciousness, and worked out the relationship between the two, we would be able to infer what conscious experiences would result from certain physical situations, which means that we would have a scientific handle on consciousness. Logical consciousness-and-physical connection plus neuroscience equals science of consciousness. Science just won't give us the initial solution. Also, many philosophical ideas have had their inspiration in scientific research, so science has already informed philosophers on this subject. For example, split-brain patients – patients who have had their corpus callosum severed, separating the two hemispheres of the brain – have produced interesting results for science, but they have also provided philosophers with something to think about regarding the unity of consciousness – something that is discussed in chapter 9 of this book.

The problem of phenomenal consciousness will not be solved with science, but there is still psychological consciousness – the easy problems – which includes explaining how people are convinced that they are phenomenally conscious. Like the problem of élan vital and life, science can get to grips with the problem of psychological consciousness without having to worry about phenomenal consciousness and whether it exists or not. It goes without saying that research into this is incredibly worthwhile. And with a function-alist assumption, this would help us to understand phenomenal consciousness.

It is not simply head-in-the-clouds philosophers who are drawn to dualistic theories. For example, hardcore scientist Christof Koch, who spent many years working on the problem of consciousness with Nobel Prize winner and co-discoverer of DNA Francis Crick, appears not to be convinced by philosophers on the subject of consciousness (2012, p. 3), and argues that scientific research is where the knowledge will be won. However, he goes on to argue for a form of dualism (see p. 152), even though this is not warranted by any scientific evidence! Welcome aboard, Christof.

The book does not end here, and that is because I will continue with the view that there is an epiphenomenal consciousness resulting from human brains. This will be until the final chapter where the assumption of physics will be turned on its head somewhat.

Chapter 6

From Brain States to Conscious States

Translation Systems

It would be convenient if there were some sort of translation system that could be used to translate physical states into conscious states. Such a system could be used to tell what anyone's conscious thoughts were by examining their brain, assuming it was examined in enough detail. But could such a system really exist? Yes – if there is a way in which conscious states are determined from physical brain states, then this is the interpretation system we are after. Therefore, if consciousness results from brain activity, a translation system must exist, even if we cannot find it or are unable to use it.

Ordinary human brains and functionally equivalent brains that are physically different are only equivalent if you look at them, or interpret them, in a certain way. There are differences between them, and only if you use the correct interpretation do they become equivalent. Even with this equivalence, there is more than one possible interpretation (see the example with the calculator in chapter 2). By accepting functionalism, you are accepting that consciousness is dependent on an interpretation of a brain state. So consciousness can be described as the 'realisation' of a possible interpretation of a physical state, even though it is not obvious how it is realised.

How do we find the interpretation system to unlock the consciousness of the brain? Can we find it by viewing the brain in isolation, or do we need the context? Daniel Dennett (1996a) believes that while there could be such an interpretation system, or a language of thought,[25] you couldn't find it simply by examining someone's brain. In the calculator example mentioned while discussing intentionality in chapter 2 of this book, you would need to know about more than just the calculator (including how it was designed to be used and interpreted) in order to find its 'correct' interpretation system. Similarly, according to Dennett, you would need more information than you could get just from the brain in isolation to find its interpretation system, from which we would find out the meaning of our thoughts and behaviour. According to Dennett, the intentionality, and therefore consciousness, of brains is dependent on how they evolved, not just how they currently are. You could, after all, seemingly assign many different meanings to our brain states and behaviour. I discussed Dennett's passage here briefly in chapter 2, but it's time to look at it in more detail:

> But what of the states and acts of those minds? What endows them with their intentionality? One popular answer is to say that these mental states and acts have meaning because they themselves, marvellously enough, are composed in a sort of language – the language of thought. Mentalese. This is a hopeless answer. It is not hopeless because there couldn't be any such system to be found in the internal goings-on in people's brains. Indeed, there could be – though any such system wouldn't be *just* like an ordinary natural language, such as English or French. It is hopeless as an answer to the question we posed, for it merely postpones the question. Let there be a language of thought. Now whence comes the meaning of *its* terms? How do you know what the sentences in your language of thought mean?[26]

and:

> [T]he brain is an artifact, and it gets whatever intentionality its parts have from their role in the ongoing economy of the larger system of which it is a part – or, in other words, from the intentions of its creator, Mother Nature (otherwise known as the process of evolution by natural selection).[27]

---

[25] The term 'Language of Thought' is Jerry Fodor's term (e.g. Fodor, 1975), and is used slightly out of context here.

[26] p. 51, italics in original

[27] pp. 52–53

It seems that what Dennett is implicitly arguing is that you could have two physically identical brains that have different conscious experiences due to having been derived differently, because the interpretation system you apply to the brain is based partly on derivation. But is this correct? Does this conclusion really follow from the possibility that there could be more than one derived meaning of a brain state? Let's not be too hasty. The interpretation system used to determine a calculator's meaning, or used by an observer to determine someone else's brain's meaning, is purely external and would not necessarily have any bearing on consciousness. The number seven on a calculator is not a conscious thought (we will take that assumption here anyway).

However, interpretation systems can translate things into more than just numbers. Just as with calculators and numbers, we can come up with as many hypothetical interpretation systems as we want for mapping brain states onto conscious states. So as with the non-conscious calculator example, there would also be many possible consciousness interpretation systems for each brain. The same rules do indeed apply in both cases. This follows from our commitment to functionalism, and that two non-physically-identical but functionally equivalent brains have the same consciousness. As said, they are only equivalent from the perspective of a particular interpretation, and we can choose many different perspectives.

It would seem that as there is more than one possible interpretation of each brain state, each brain should actually have multiple conscious minds arising from it, unless there is a 'correct' interpretation system. Intrinsic intentionality would provide this, but we have already dismissed that. This brings us back to Dennett, and the possibility that derivation is important. So can derivation stop us from having many conscious minds arising from our brains?

One of the major points that comes up in discussions of intentionality is whether causation, or derivation, is an important factor. According to what Dennett says here it would be, but Searle would argue not (certainly not when it comes to 'real' intentionality). Before we go any further, let's look a bit more at causation's possible role in intentionality.

American philosopher Hilary Putnam (1981, pp. 1–3) uses the example of an ant walking in the sand and in doing so drawing a line, which, by chance, happens to look like Winston Churchill. Is this line a representation of Winston Churchill? Putnam says that most people would say not, as there was no intention (in the everyday sense of the word) to draw Churchill. There was also no causal link between Churchill and the drawing in the sand. Intuitively it would not seem that this picture is about Churchill. This implies that the object itself and its properties in isolation are not enough to determine what it is about. Someone could make a drawing identical to the ant's that is of Winston Churchill. In this situation, there would be a causal link between Winston Churchill and the picture. The way Winston Churchill looked would have caused the way the picture looked. We would then have two identical physical states with potentially different aboutness or intentionality.

But is it the causal link that is relevant here? Someone could take the ant's picture and use it as a representation of Churchill. Would it not then become about Churchill? It could, but in this situation there would actually be a causal link between Churchill and the intentionality of this object. The resemblance between Churchill and the picture is what would cause the person to pick it out. If Churchill had not existed, no-one would take a picture and say it was of him. In this case, it would seem that causation is important in our everyday understanding of what something is about. But is there a significance to this beyond semantics and word games? Does it make a difference when it comes to determining the conscious states of brains? That is what is important here.

Swampman

According to Donald Davidson (1987), the derivation of a brain is an important factor in determining its actual conscious states, not just the best way for an observer to interpret the brain states externally. He gives an example of an exact replica of him without his history:

> Suppose lightning strikes a dead tree in a swamp; I am standing nearby. My body is reduced to its elements, while entirely by coinci-

dence (and out of different molecules) the tree is turned into my physical replica. My replica, The Swampman, moves exactly as I did; according to its nature it departs the swamp, encounters and seems to recognize my friends, and appears to return their greetings in English. It moves into my house and seems to write articles on radical interpretation. No one can tell the difference.

But there *is* a difference. My replica can't recognize my friends; it can't *re*cognize anything, since it never cognized anything in the first place. It can't know my friends' names (though of course it seems to), it can't remember my house. It can't mean what I do by the word 'house', for example, since the sound 'house' it makes was not learned in a context that would give it the right meaning – or any meaning at all. Indeed, I don't see how my replica can be said to mean anything by the sounds it makes, nor to have any thoughts.[28]

According to Davidson, although Swampman is physically identical to a specific human, it would have no thoughts, and presumably therefore no conscious thoughts. All of the utterances that it made, which would make sense to us as words, would be meaningless noises to Swampman. This is because Swampman and all of its brain states have not been derived in a meaningful way, which, according to Davidson, means that Swampman would have no intentionality and no consciousness.

Intuitively, to me at least, it would seem that Swampman would have exactly the same conscious experiences as Davidson, simply because he is physically identical. But Swampman does not have the same derivation as the original Davidson, having been formed randomly. So if (as Dennett and Davidson would argue) derivation is important, Swampman's conscious experiences would not be the same as the original Davidson's.

Let's clear this up. Does it really make sense to say that Swampman would not have the same conscious thoughts as Davidson? They are physically identical, so their conscious states would have to be identical unless there are some non-physical properties given to an object by its history, which play a role in consciousness production. These non-physical properties would make Davidson's view a form of dualism, and one with not much

---

[28] pp. 443–444, italics in original

plausibility. If we are taking the consciousness/brain link seriously, then consciousness should be fixed by the physical make-up of the brain, regardless of derivation. There would be no possible way of finding any difference between physically identical brains of different derivation, so there would be no reason to believe that there is a difference.

In accepting Davidson's view, we would be saying that the brain has some sort of memory of the past that isn't represented in any physical system – a form of epiphenomenal homeopathy. Consciousness would be determined by a combination of physical make-up and this non-physical memory. It would be a very messy theory without any good reason that I can see for believing it. Some may immediately draw parallels with epiphenomenalist dualism. However, with the version of epiphenomenalism that I have described, the properties of consciousness are completely deter-mined by the current properties of an existent physical system. The dualism implied by Davidson's views requires access to the past, and non-physical differences between physically identical objects.

It is also worth pointing out that if you went far enough back, you would find that the meaning of Davidson's own thoughts is not rooted in anything with real meaning anyway. Evolution by natural selection and the laws of physics have no intentionality and are completely blind processes. I'm not sure at what point real meaning is supposed to have started.

The only conclusion we can draw is that derivation does not have any relevance in determining conscious states, which means that Swampman would have exactly the same consciousness as Davidson. But derivation was supposed to be a way of determining which interpretation system is responsible for consciousness. Without it, we are still left with the problem that there are many possible interpretation systems that we could apply to a brain, and there does not seem to be an obvious way of deciding which one is correct. Perhaps there are multiple conscious minds per brain.

You might think that the idea of a conscious mind being derived from an interpretation of a brain state, and indeed just one of many possible interpretations, is a bizarre direction for me to be going in. But this is forced upon us if we are taking a functional view of the mind. And this is exactly the problem that Dennett and Davidson have been addressing, even if they have not been quite so explicit.

Psychophysical Laws to the Rescue?

David Chalmers (1996) believes that it is logically possible for there to exist a being physically identical to him that sees blue where he sees red. This is an example of the famous inverted spectrum idea that I briefly mentioned in chapter 4. Perhaps you have wondered yourself if other people see the same colours differently to you, but no-one could ever know because we all give the same labels to them. Chalmers's point here goes beyond that, by saying that this could even happen among physically identical beings (pp. 100–101).

According to the multiple-consciousnesses-per-brain idea that I have suggested, there could actually be a mind associated with Chalmers's brain that sees blue where another mind associated with his brain sees red, but without the need for two beings with separate but physically identical brains.

Chalmers, however, believes that each brain does in fact only have one conscious mind, even though he accepts that there are many logically possible minds for it to be picked from. According to Chalmers, there are psychophysical laws that determine the conscious states of a brain. Chalmers says that these are natural laws rather than logical laws, and could be different in different universes, leading to cases of physically identical beings with different conscious experiences. This is because, according to Chalmers, consciousness does not logically supervene on the physical (it is not logically implied by the physical), but only does so naturally. This seems to fly in the face of his 'dancing qualia' argument for functionalism that I discussed in chapter 4. Imagine a teleport that can immediately flip you back and forth between two universes with different psychophysical laws. In Chalmers's own terms, your qualia would dance in front of your eyes without you noticing anything. His point is that the qualia would be constant for a given set of psychophysical laws, so would be fixed in a given world or even universe, but this variation seems just as unpalatable to me.

Anyway, Chalmers's idea of different possible psychophysical laws seems to agree with the idea that I have presented that multiple minds could come from each brain, except that he has his laws to keep one mind per brain.

However, I do not think that the two ideas are coming from the same direction. Chalmers views the brain as a system functioning in a specific way, and from what I understand he only considers there to be one interpretation of its functioning, or one relevant one at least. Chalmers thinks that even with this one interpretation, there are still many possible minds, such as the one that sees blue where he sees red, in a universe with different psychophysical laws. My point is that there are many ways of interpreting the brain's functioning, and, as a result, many possible minds. In fact, I would not agree with the conclusion that for a specific interpretation there would be more than one possible mind. Each mind is simply *the* realisation of a particular interpretation.

You cannot divorce the functional state from the conscious state associated with it, particularly if you are going by a functional theory of consciousness, as Chalmers is. So you cannot simply decide that identical functional states can actually result in two different conscious states for two different people, even if they are in different universes, on the basis that it seems plausible at first sight. When Dennett (1991, pp. 389–398) is 'disqualifying' qualia, he makes the point that by inverting your colour qualia (so that, for example, you might see red as blue and blue as red with all the other corresponding changes, as in Chalmers's examples), you would create more problems, as your reactive dispositions to the colours would change as well. What a colour looks like is not an independent stand-alone phenomenon.

Dennett does a good job of showing that these qualia are not elemental (as I discussed in chapter 1), and that by playing with your colour experiences, you cannot help but affect your other experiences as well. You cannot isolate and vary an individual quale and have no functional effect elsewhere. If you varied your colour qualia, you would also have to vary other qualia to compensate for your change in how you relate to those qualia (e.g. so that the colour of blood is still the same as the colour for danger and invokes all the same thoughts) and then more again to compensate for those changes and so on. It seems that you would end up, metaphorically speaking, 'rotating' your whole conscious experience as one, leaving it unchanged. After the first change, you might start off by seeing red as blue, but when all the other changes had been made, it would look red again.

As an example of a full rotation, imagine a being that is an exact mirror image of a human in a world that is a mirror image of Earth. Would this being's mind have the same visual experiences as us, or would they be reversed? To make the point clearer, imagine if the mirror-image being found itself thrown into our world. It would look at exactly the same physical objects as us, except that its brain would be a mirror image. So of course it would perceive everything the other way round from us, and be greatly confused. So now imagine again the brain that is maintained as a mirror image entirely, and not thrown into our world. Everything would cancel out, and the experience would be the same as ours, not a mirror image.

Here is what Chalmers (1996) has to say about inverting the spectrum, leaving the 'warmth' of thoughts and reactions dissociated:

> First, there does not seem to be anything *incoherent* about the notion of such a dissociation (e.g., cool phenomenology with warm reactions), although it is admittedly an odd idea. Second, instead of mapping red precisely onto blue and vice versa, one can imagine that these are mapped onto slightly different colors. For example, red might be mapped onto a "warm" version of blue [...] or even onto color not in our color space at all.[29]

It is interesting that Chalmers allows a dissociation between phenomenal and psychological consciousness cognition here, even though it was his dislike of the concept that drew him towards functionalism in the first place. If you allow a slight dissociation, why not take it to its logical conclusion and say that any functional state can be associated with any conscious state and do away with functionalism altogether?

---

[29] p. 100, italics in original

It is also not merely warmth or coolness that determines what a colour looks like. We have various reactions to each colour, but it is the functional state in its entirety (rather than just one aspect, such as 'warmth') that determines the phenomenal properties of a colour. There is every reason to believe that this pinpoints it exactly. The conscious mind is simply a passive reflection of the functional architecture of the brain. It has no independently variable properties of its own.

Chalmers considers swapping seeing red with seeing blue, because as far as conscious experiences go, they are fairly similar. But what about a being that had its red experience swapped with the sudden thought that it was late for work? This may sound ridiculous, but I would argue that this is merely a difference of degree. Swapping red with blue is equally absurd, but just a smaller change so not as obviously absurd. Of course, in reality people may experience colours differently from each other, but I would argue that there would also have to be a corresponding functional difference and that we could find this out empirically. In this sense, even zombic materialists could reasonably talk about the possibility of inverted psychologically conscious states. But this does not mean that there is a hard problem of psychological consciousness, since it would all be measurable.

If we take the view that there is one standard way to interpret the brain, then it seems that there is only one mind resultant from it, and no other possible mind that sees blue where you would see red. A different mind requires a different interpretation. A mind is simply the conscious isomorph of a particular interpretation of a brain state. Perhaps some people might see this isomorphism as very close to a form of materialism where the functional brain state simply is the conscious state. Close, but not close enough. Consciousness is not a physical state itself, but an abstraction from it – resulting from a pattern or interpretation of it. The conscious state itself is non-physical and an impotent by-product.

But the problem here remains unsolved. It does still seem that we have multiple possible interpretations for each brain state, leaving the possibility of multiple minds per brain.

Another Solution?

Perhaps some interpretation systems are more arbitrary than others. What would aliens make of us and our human languages? They could interpret our behaviour in any number of arbitrary ways, but I think most people would agree that they would be likely to get to the bottom of most of what we do and interpret it in some sensible way. Obviously talking about these aliens creates a further problem of how to interpret what the aliens are doing and how to interpret their interpretations, but that does not necessarily mean that the whole thing falls apart there and then, or at least I will give it the benefit of the doubt for now.

William Poundstone (1988) discusses how to decode ciphers, and how it is possible to get to the bottom of some, whereas if you just have a long string of one letter, it could equally mean anything.

> A ciphertext of *iiii* ... has the minimum possible entropy, far less than any real language. Usually, a cipher has as much or more entropy than plaintext. When the entropy is less [...] it means that part of the message information has been shunted into the ciphering system. The ciphertext is ambiguous. Deciphering it depends on information not in the ciphertext: a key or the ability of the original author to reconstruct the message from an equivocal ciphertext.[30]

However, any 'decipherable' ciphertext could still be deciphered into any text in English, if you came up with a suitable interpretation system. And no information in the ciphertext itself can unequivocally tell you that you have found the correct solution. The 'correct' answer always depends on information outside what you are trying to interpret, even if there might be one solution that sticks out at you. To talk about some ciphertexts as containing all the information themselves and others as having information shunted into the ciphering system is overly simplistic and not entirely accurate. A ciphertext can never objectively contain all the information needed in order to decipher it in one specific way.

---

[30] p. 217, non-bracketed ellipsis and italics in original

Douglas Hofstadter (1979) talks about intrinsic meaning. While clearly there is no such thing in a literal sense (as in intrinsic intentionality), some meanings do seem to take less effort to extract, and this is a similar concept to what Poundstone is talking about.

> That is why the meaning is part of the test itself: it acts upon intelligence in a predictable way. Generally, we can say: meaning is part of an object to the extent that it acts upon intelligence in a predictable way.[31]

However, there is still no way of saying that one interpretation system is objectively correct for something waiting to be interpreted, even if we, as intelligent beings, may all converge on the same answer. And although one interpretation system may arguably be simpler or less arbitrary than the others, this still does not mean that it is the 'correct' one, or that it is the only one that will somehow produce consciousness in a brain. It seems that the ways around the problem of multiple minds per brain are just intrinsic intentionality in disguise, or require the creation of extra arbitrary laws.

Multiple Minds It Is

Because of these considerations, I would argue that having multiple consciousnesses per brain is a more viable theory than having exactly one consciousness per brain. Of course, it is intuitive for us to believe that our brains have one consciousness associated with them, but this does not necessarily make it true. Indeed, it may initially seem a violation of Ockham's Razor to talk about many minds being associated with a brain, but there is no contradiction to this, and having just one consciousness would mean having extra arbitrary laws to determine which interpretation system is correct, so I see that as more of a violation. Simpler laws can lead to more 'stuff', so this is no contradiction. Apart from zombic materialism, the many minds route actually seems to be the simplest and most plausible way to go. After all, why should some brain interpretation systems be correct, or 'active', and not others?

---

[31] p. 165

Consciousness is just the realisation of an interpretation – a sort of extraction of a meaning – of a physical brain state and is, therefore, not physical, and cannot have any effects in the outside world. And given that these different conscious minds caused by different interpretations would not interfere with the outside world or with each other, different conscious minds could exist simultaneously without creating any philosophical headaches such as causal overdetermination. Even if we had not previously concluded in favour of epiphenomenalism, we would have to now. There are seemingly many conscious minds arising from your brain, many of which may think they have control, but are all impotent by-products of brain activity, and are merely spectators. Otherwise we would be left with this causal overdetermination, with all the minds simultaneously controlling the body. Concluding in favour of functionalism forces one into epiphenomenalism, since functioning has to be interpreted, and this interpretation has no physical basis, and has to come from outside.

How these interpretation systems could be realised is not clear. There does not appear to be an outside system that can interpret the goings-on in our physical universe, although there is a sort of equality if all possible interpretations are equally realised. I think a more accurate term than 'functionalism' for my stance on the problem of consciousness is 'interpretationalism'. Functionalism is included within it – two objects that are functionally identical by a particular interpretation system would be consciously identical using that interpretation system – but 'interpretationalism' is a more general term.

When looking at a brain, someone could look at things that we would consider irrelevant in our interpretation system, and use it in their own interpretation system, such as something in the nature of the neurons that we would not normally consider in a functional sense. We can pin down what we would consider to be a sensible interpretation, and so a mind worth looking at, at least to an extent. Any sensible interpretation system would be one that ends up with the same interpretation for a human brain and a functionally equivalent silicon chip brain. Obviously if we are functionalists, then we would seemingly commit to this anyway, but more generally we are interpretationalists, and a bizarre interpreter could consider them not to be interpretationally equivalent.

Let's reconsider the calculator example from chapter 2, and assume, for the sake of argument, that the realisation of our interpretation of a calculator does have some rudimentary consciousness. Would the number-doubling interpretation provide a different consciousness? Possibly, but then possibly not. Arbitrarily defining digits in a different way does not necessarily change anything. Think back to the spectrum inversion from earlier in this chapter. Red and blue were reversed, but then to compensate for all of the colour changes, everything else needed to be changed, and the relative positions ended up the same as before. Red had become red again by the back door, whatever label an outsider might decide to apply to it, and perhaps the same would apply here.

Of course, instead of taking each digit to mean twice its intended value, we could muddle them up in a more complex fashion. For example, '1' could mean 'six', '2' could mean 'five', '3' could mean 'eight' and so on. But then the operators +, -, x and / would have to take on very strange and complex meanings for the maths to work. This bigger change could possibly avoid the interpretational equivalence.

Likewise, the brain's functioning could be interpreted in as bizarre a manner as we like. However, the fact that there may be many conscious minds arising from your brain is not necessarily as bad as you may think. Many of the minds would come from quite bizarre interpretations and could well result in what would probably be best described as conscious noise.

By the time we get rid of all the interpretations that result in conscious noise and interpretations that fail to meet our functional requirements based on the equivalence of silicon brains, we may be left with very little. It may be that there is only one interpretation and one consciousness left that is worth talking about. In that case it would not be worth worrying about any extra conscious minds that your brain may have. They would just be epiphenomenal hot air. Of course, if any interpretation system is valid, then arguably all possible minds, including ordered minds that happen not to reflect outside reality, could be created from a single brain's activity.

However, because of the strained nature of some of these interpretation systems, they are likely to result in minds that are only fleetingly ordered and that return to disorder after the shortest of moments. It could also be that interpretations that result in an ordered mind that reflects the real world statistically outnumber the more bizarre minds to a great enough degree to render the bizarre minds a negligible part of reality. I will return to the point of the statistical likelihood of minds in the final chapter.

The next few chapters will continue with the assumption that we have a single consciousness worth talking about, even if only because it makes the discussion easier. But I will return to the issue of multiple minds in chapters 9 and 12, each from different perspectives.

Chapter 7

Loose Ends

More on intentionality

Having discussed Swampman and various other arguments, we are in a clearer position on the notion of intentionality.

There are philosophers who have spent a great deal of time and effort debating what it means for something to be about something else. According to some, meaning is determined, at least in part, by derivation, or causation. Swampman was an example of where this could be made relevant in terms of a real difference being made – a difference to consciousness. But we have found this claim to be untenable, as an implausible epiphenomenon would have to be created. It does not matter how an object came about.

What philosophical significance can we attach to intentionality? Regardless of the intentionality or aboutness you may consider an object to have, nothing philosophically important rests on it. All objects, brains included, only have derived, observer-relative, or non-philosophically-important intentionality. It is the only sort of intentionality there is that relates to physical objects. When you make claims as to what a physical brain state (as opposed to the conscious state) is about, there is no objective truth to the matter. For example, you might say that someone's brain state is about a horse because it resulted after the subject saw a horse, and that another, physically identical, brain state is not about a horse because that particular brain formed randomly, like Swampman. But no, the brain states are identical in every way. Any difference that you may assign to them regarding intentionality, or indeed anything else, is just a labelling system for you.

Of course, what matters more to us than the brain state is the conscious state that comes about due to that brain state. And to an extent the same applies here. Two identical conscious states are identical regardless of how they formed. Using the example from the paragraph above, you could argue that one conscious state is about a horse and the other not. But any difference is in you and how you relate to the conscious states, not in the conscious states themselves. It has often been claimed that for a thought to be conscious, it has to be conscious of or about something, but consciousness is simply a self-contained phenomenal state. However, it certainly seems to us that our conscious states are about something. Indeed, it could be argued that a conscious state is objectively about some abstract concept (and so differs from physical objects in this respect), but it certainly is not about a specific existent object in any objective sense.

You can argue all you like whether a line drawn in the sand by an ant really is a picture of Winston Churchill, or whether Swampman is really a man, or whether Swamphammer[32] is really a hammer, but it won't change anything. You would be playing word games, and it is simply a matter of what definitions you choose to use.

If, as in Rosenthal's HOT theory discussed in chapter 1, conscious states have to have other higher-order states that are about them, we can reasonably ask whether these higher-order states are objectively about the state that they make conscious. I would argue that if these states were truly separate from each other, then the same rules would apply as do with any other form of intentionality, so the higher-order thought is not objectively about the thought it would make conscious. But of course your thoughts and your thoughts about your thoughts aren't entirely separate from each other, and so there is no clear dividing line between a higher-order thought and an extension of the original thought.

There may be areas of the brain that have a higher-than-usual level of communication between them at a given time, and this may correspond to when someone says that they have a thought about another thought, or they may say that their original thought has gained wider coverage. This is similar to the discussion of why qualia

---

[32] Thank you to Denis McManus for bringing up this example in discussion. I do not know whether he made it up himself.

cannot be said to be elemental and Dennett's example of the acquired taste of beer that I discussed in chapter 1. There is no objectively correct answer to the question of whether it is someone's taste qualia or their dispositions to those qualia that change when they come to like the taste of beer. Similarly, there is no objectively correct answer in this case to the question of whether there are two thoughts or one thought that has gained wider coverage. This is another reason why the HOT theory cannot be entirely accurate. There is also the question of how full a representation of the original thought the higher-order thought has to have, how accurate it needs to be (you can be wrong about your thoughts), and how well connected it needs to be to the original thought. For example, I could have a thought about one of your thoughts, but I doubt you would agree that this would make it conscious. These all come in degrees, so there can be no simple answer.

Daniel Dennett and Definitions

We have discussed Daniel Dennett and the significance he places on derivation regarding intentionality. So what would he make of Swampman? From what we have discussed of him so far, it would appear that he would say that Swampman does not have the same consciousness as Davidson. But he does not say this. He does not even consider the thought experiment to be worth discussing:

> Smiling demons, cow-sharks, Blockheads, and Swampmen are all, some philosophers think, logically possible, even if they are not nomologically possible, and these philosophers think this is important. I do not. Why should the truth-maker question cast its net this wide? Because, I gather, otherwise its answer doesn't tell us about the *essence* of the topic in question. But who believes in real essences of this sort nowadays? Not I.[33]

Isn't this escaping the issue? Maybe, but it becomes easier to understand Dennett's position on this when you understand his views on consciousness as a whole.

---

[33]   1996b, pp. 76–77, italics in original

Dennett doesn't deny the existence of consciousness, but this is because he seems to use a different definition from everyone else. Chalmers (1996, pp. 189–191) and Searle (1998, pp. 97–115), to name two, have both pointed this out. Arguably, Dennett is effectively a zombic materialist, but defines consciousness in such a way that it fits into his system.

Recall Dennett's comparison of consciousness and health, discussed in chapter 5. According to Dennett, consciousness is nothing more than our idea of psychological consciousness – not in the way in which it turns out that phenomenal and psychological consciousness are the same thing, but in that psychological consciousness is all we need to worry about from the start. And remember, this is the psychological consciousness that is not actually conscious in our sense of the term, at least not by definition alone. From *Consciousness Explained* (1991):

> "raw feels," "sensa," "phenomenal qualities," "intrinsic properties of conscious experiences," "the qualitative content of mental states," and, of course, "qualia," the term I will use. There are subtle differences in how these terms have been defined, but I'm going to ride roughshod over them. In the previous chapter I seemed to be denying that there are *any* such properties, and for once what seems so *is* so. I *am* denying that there are any such properties.[34]

According to Dennett, once you have found out why people psychologically believe in consciousness, you have solved the problem. He ignores the idea of a possibly separate phenomenal consciousness, the sort that we are concerned with, and simply defines consciousness to be psychological consciousness. He is concerned only with the 'easy' problems. According to our definitions, a being with only psychological consciousness would be a zombie, since it is not actually conscious. But since, according to Dennett, this is the only sort of consciousness, he considers the idea of zombies absurd. It is as if consciousness and zombies have both been shifted back one level, so that zombies have nowhere left to go. Consciousness shifts from phenomenal to psychological using Dennett's definitions, but

---

[34]   p. 372, italics in original

zombies are already at the psychological level. There is not a 'lower' level of consciousness than psychological, so zombies could not possibly exist. Of course zombies are absurd if you adopt that position.

While discussing a functional definition of consciousness, Chalmers (1996) says:

> One might as well define "world peace" as "a ham sandwich." Achieving world peace becomes much easier, but it is a hollow achievement.[35]

And good for him. But what does this have to do with Dennett's views on Swampman? Well, since Dennett is using a functional, non-phenomenal definition of consciousness, he can simply define which things are conscious and which things aren't, without worrying whether they 'truly are'. There is no fundamental truth as to what is conscious, merely definitions, once you eliminate phenomenal consciousness. Which objects are conscious would occupy the same area in philosophical space as whether a line in the sand is a picture of Winston Churchill.

This is why Swampman is not really worth discussing, according to him. It is not a matter of trying to work out what its conscious-ness would be like phenomenally, but just a matter of deciding which category to put Swampman in, which wouldn't be worth-while, as there is nothing philosophical at stake. Why categorise objects that will never exist? Dennett's definitions are there to describe everyday phenomena, so there would be no point in him modifying his definitions to include such hypothetical examples. It would be like us discussing whether Swamphammer is really a hammer; no truths would be uncovered.

So when Dennett talks about derived intentionality, it is because he is talking about the best way to define the intentionality of a system. It doesn't mean that he thinks that there is some fundamen-tal difference between the original Davidson and Swampman. His views on derivation would seem to imply that their consciousness is

---

[35]   p. 105

different, but Dennett apparently does not require his definitions to be so rigorous as to include all possible objects.

It is only if you consider the problem of consciousness to be more than a matter of definitions that you need to worry about Swampman. If Dennett believed in the type of consciousness we are discussing – phenomenal consciousness – he would have to address Swampman. There would be a truth to be discovered: does Swampman have the same phenomenal consciousness as Davidson? You couldn't simply define this question away, unless you want to define 'world peace' as 'a ham sandwich'.

Having said all of that, the idea of Swampman might not be so easily dismissible as implausible. Similar to Swampman is the Boltzmann Brain. Empty space is not entirely uniform, and quantum mechanics predicts that particles randomly pop in and out of existence all the time. The vast majority of these formations have no complex form. However, over enough space and time, objects with greater complexity will randomly appear, including fully-formed human brains complete with thoughts and memories. These are Boltzmann Brains. This isn't just a philosopher's thought experiment, but something taken seriously by many physicists. So whether a randomly formed brain, or indeed Swampman, is conscious is something that may need to be addressed. I will return to the idea of Boltzmann Brains in the final chapter.

The Blindness of Physics and the Purpose Delusion

The laws of physics are blind, and I think that it is important to emphasise this. They have no purpose. They simply cause matter to interact in a certain way without any vision of an end result. And they are blind in any system that they are acting in, whether it be a clock or a human brain.

Simple laws can lead to complex processes, such as the existence of human life. Evolution by natural selection is a blind process that has worked over millions of years to produce us. Most people would not have a problem in accepting this. But most people would say that we humans, as a result of the blind process of evolution, do not act blindly ourselves, but have real purpose in our behaviour.

But we have fallen into a trap here. It is a very attractive and intuitive notion that our behaviour has purpose, to the point where most people have probably not even considered the existence of an alternative. However, the laws of physics are acting as blindly in us as they are in anything else. There is no meaning or purpose in anything physical that happens. Any meaning has to come from the outside. Meaning is simply an outside interpretation of events, not a part of the events. This is to say that, like consciousness, purpose is not part of the physical world, and can only be part of a mind that is outside the physical system. Of course, it is quite a natural trap to fall into, and you have joined distinguished company, including biologist and professional atheist Richard Dawkins, as well as most of the rest of the world's population. I have tried to find a quote from Dawkins on this but this is the best I could come up with:

> I have devoted a whole book (*Unweaving the Rainbow*) to ultimate meaning, to the poetry of science, and to rebutting, specifically and at length, the charge of nihilistic negativity, so I shall restrain myself here.[36]

No, go on! I could not find a quote summing up his position in *Unweaving the Rainbow* (1998), but regardless, I doubt he would consider me to be misrepresenting his views by saying that he thinks that our behaviour is purposeful. He would probably argue that I was missing the point by trying to sum this whole issue up with a specific quote anyway.

Of course, an observer (or the epiphenomenal mind of a physical observer) might be totally convinced after watching us that we are displaying purposeful behaviour. It seems so specifically geared towards achieving certain tasks. How can this be an illusion?

Evolution by natural selection has determined which behaviours survive and which do not. Genes that cause behaviours that in turn result in successful survival and reproduction are the ones that get passed down into future generations. Of course, the whole process is blind: both evolution and the behaviour that it selects. But it can all give the illusion that humans and other animals are doing things *for*

---

[36] 2006, p. 214, italics in original

the achievement of certain goals. But they are not doing anything *for* anything. There is no purpose; the laws of physics are merely playing out, and certain patterns, including complex behaviours, are more likely than others to occur for any given set of laws. Evolution itself can look purposeful, but this is generally considered to be an illusion. I am just taking this to the next logical step.

As I have pointed out (chapter 6), behaviour can be interpreted in more than one way. Some of these interpretations may appear strained or arbitrary, but they are no less 'correct' than any other. And by using one of these strained interpretations, you could well end up seeing a different purpose in our behaviour or no purpose at all.

Purposeful behaviour requires a potent consciousness, and you won't find one of those in any physical object. You could argue that an epiphenomenal conscious mind has a purpose of sorts, however. There is the intention to act on the world in a physical way, but the mind is deluded into thinking it has the power to do so, and so it is not a purpose that results in any action.

So to conclude, any meaning or purpose or intentionality that can be seen in human behaviour has to come from outside. Meaning is epiphenomenal, and so is purpose. It is easy to think that we have evolved purpose and meaning, and that these have helped us to survive in our environment. But this does not stop it from being wrong. To borrow from Dawkins himself (2006), we can now add the Purpose Delusion to the God Delusion (if, of course, you agree with his stance on God).

Do You Know You're Conscious?

We have already seen that it is only incorrect reasoning that leads us to believe that we are conscious, so it might seem that we cannot know we are conscious, even if we are. But this is not necessarily the case.

Perhaps the best way of understanding this is to look at the physical (or psychological) side of a human and the conscious (epiphenomenal) side as separate entities. The physical side of the human incorrectly reasons that it has consciousness. The conscious side would then passively hold the correct view that it is conscious, which could be seen as a sort of knowledge. But the conscious side is epiphenomenal and is completely reliant on the physical side in order to gain that knowledge. The knowledge is not self-reinforcing in any way, being epiphenomenal, so this knowledge could be lost.

It might seem to you that a less intelligent being might not have the capacity to see that it is conscious, but once it becomes sufficiently advanced to see it, there is no way back. Once consciousness is seen, it cannot be unseen. It may indeed be true that in most cases a being advanced enough to see itself as conscious will never go back. But it is clear that this would not be the result of seeing consciousness itself, as I have explained, but because of other considerations (see the discussion of the Paradox of Phenomenal Judgement for one such account, in chapter 3). The physical side of the being does all the reasoning, and concludes that it is conscious, despite having no access to any consciousness. So, if a being that does believe itself to be conscious then advances even further intellectually, and becomes more capable of seeing things objectively, it may decide that it has no consciousness at all, however counterintuitive that may be. Of course, this being may then end up as an evolutionary dead end! Having said that, one's intellectual beliefs do not necessarily inform one's habit-driven day-to-day behaviour.

The point is that we are wrong to reason that we are conscious, even if through our doing so, our consciousness gains the correct knowledge that it is conscious. However, Chalmers (1996) argues that he knows he is conscious and is justified in his belief (the 'he' being his conscious mind):

> It might still be objected, "But the belief would still have been formed even if the experience had been absent!" To this, the answer is, "So what?" In *this* case, I have *evidence* for my belief, namely my immediate acquaintance with experience. In a different case, that evidence is absent. To note that in a different case the belief might have been formed in the absence of the evidence is not to say that the evidence does not justify the belief in this case. I *know* I am conscious, and the knowledge is based solely on my immediate experience. To say that experience makes no difference to my psychological functioning is not to say that the experience makes no

difference to *me*.[37]

But if an epiphenomenal consciousness holds a belief, then I would say it is wrong to talk about justification at all, in terms of being either right or wrong, since it is merely an impotent reflection of a psychological belief. The epiphenomenal mind has done no reasoning itself, and its beliefs are just fed to it. It cannot be justified or unjustified in any of its properties. I would also say that Chalmers lacks objectivity in saying that he knows he is conscious, since it is not his consciousness writing the book. It is the physical Chalmers, who has no access to any consciousness. Similarly, it is not my consciousness writing this book, but I am writing it from the perspective of someone who wants to know (at least psychologically) what properties consciousness might have if it does exist, rather than someone who claims to know that it does.

So while it does seem to be possible to know that you are conscious (depending on your definition of 'knowledge'), this can only be as a result of incorrect psychological reasoning, unless we one day find a logical connection between the physical and consciousness. A belief in consciousness could be seen to be similar to a belief in God. Many religious people claim to know that God exists because they have experienced him personally, but cannot present any evidence to anyone else. Other people might write off this claim as deluded and invoke Dawkins's God Delusion. The same argument can be used against our belief in consciousness, except that everyone suffers from this delusion, so there is no-one left to point this out to us. So in addition to the God Delusion and the Purpose Delusion, we also have the Consciousness Delusion.

The Science of Consciousness – Inferring the Experiences of Others and the Other Minds Problem

As I said in chapter 5, if at some point it can be shown logically that consciousness does follow from physical processing, then the logical relationship, along with our empirical data, can form a science of consciousness and a better understanding of our own conscious-

---

[37] p. 198, italics in original

ness. The logical connection without the empirical data would not be enough to understand consciousness, because the processes would be far too complex to work out from first principles. Analogously, we cannot work out the science of weather systems directly from the laws of quantum mechanics.

Even without the logical connection (which we currently do not have), you can still make inferences from your own (alleged) consciousness. If you have a conscious mind resulting from your brain, then with more advanced technology, you could examine your brain and see the way in which your conscious thoughts seem to follow from it. You could then make inferences about how consciousness results from brains in general, and make an estimate of other people's experiences. This is effectively what scientists do now anyway – they try to find what they call the 'neural correlates of consciousness'. It's just that our understanding of it is currently not that advanced. Examining your brain properly requires a great understanding!

It doesn't matter that we don't have any empirical evidence for the consciousness you are looking for. All you really need to do is consider psychological consciousness, which we can be sure does exist. There is certainly nothing philosophically mysterious about psychological consciousness, and we are going by the view that phenomenal consciousness is merely a reflection of that. So if you record and understand what someone is experiencing psychologically (according to a reasonable interpretation system), your epiphenomenal mind should then understand it in phenomenal terms, since one is a reflection of the other. If we can psychologically understand what someone is psychologically thinking (which seems reasonable), then we should be able to phenomenally understand what they are phenomenally thinking. It does not matter that the phenomenal understanding cannot be directly communicated – it is enough for you to know that you have it!

It is not worth worrying too much about the possibility of multiple conscious minds existing (discussed in chapter 6). If you think of yourself as an epiphenomenal mind resulting from your brain, and you use recorded output to infer other people's experiences, then it does not matter too much if you are only inferring the experiences of minds resulting from the same interpretation system as your mind. At least it is a start, and as discussed, there may only be one 'sensible' mind that comes from each brain.

However, having a way of inferring and recording other people's experiences will still not solve all of our problems. Each conscious experience is very complex; a list of what colour experiences someone has in each part of their visual field, along with what sounds they can hear, the feeling of their feet on the floor, what they are thinking about and everything else would surely be far too complex for one person to digest. You would really only be able to understand small parts of their conscious experience at any given time, and even then probably not in great detail.

Then there is the problem of when the experience, which could be of a non-human, is nothing like anything that you have experienced yourself, so maybe there would be nothing that could be recorded on paper that would help you to understand it. For example, could we really understand what it is like to be a bat?

If understanding the minds of others means being able to experience their experiences, we are always going to struggle to get inside the mind of a bat because we have completely different mental structures, so we could not simply think its thoughts. Using printed records, we could probably only understand the conscious thoughts of other beings that have similar experiences to us in any great detail. But I think this at least shows that it is not impossible in principle to have some understanding of the thoughts of a being that is not you (something which may seem obvious anyway), and from there everything is arguably a matter of degree. Also, consider going back in time to see your old (or young, if you want to look at it that way) self. The 'you' then is not the same as you now, but you should be able to understand at least some of your old thoughts quite well.

Regarding third-person techniques, if we really could understand everything that was going on in a bat's brain all at once (or the brain of any other being), it might be possible that we would be able to understand their experiences in an equivalent way (as I also suggested with Mary the Colour Scientist in chapter 3), although this is speculative. Of course, we may then wonder if our experiences of their experiences really are the same, but if they result from the same brain pattern, they should be functionally and interpretationally isomorphic, and as argued in the previous chapter, this should be enough to make them the same. But it would involve a full physical understanding, which will not realistically happen (certainly not any time soon), and it would probably require an all-at-once understanding of a brain state, rather than being able to work through it all at your own pace. To effectively contain the mind of another being in your own mind would require you to have considerably more brain power than the other being, and we would probably hit our limits long before we reached bats.

For those of us lacking the ability to swallow all the physical information from another brain at once, we can possibly solve our problems with an 'experience producer'. It is not something that currently exists (clearly), but that need not stop us. What this does is stimulate our neurons to produce the correct conscious experience, thus doing away with the need for us to learn the information from the outside; the information would be presented to us internally in an all-at-once manner. This would be far more efficient, allowing us to understand the consciousness of brains more complex than previously. Obviously we don't have our neurons in the right arrangements to be capable of certain conscious experiences, including bat-like experiences. However, the experience producer does not just stimulate our existing neurons, but can also work as an extra module with its own artificial neurons to provide us with all the hardware we need for the experiences we are after.

There would then be the problem of remembering the experiences once the module has been removed, since our own brain may not be able to record such alien experiences properly, and much of the experience would come from the external module. In many cases this would not be such a problem, such as when we are experiencing the thoughts of another human, and we should still be able to retain at least some of the flavour of the bat-like experiences, since they would still involve many of the neurons in our brains as well as the artificial ones. It is difficult to know how much we could retain, however.

There is a further problem: would it be us having the experiences, or does adding the experience producer, with its artificial neurons, create a separate individual? The general problem of personal identity is discussed at length in chapter 10, but there is no need to worry about it too much now. Certainly what you retain after the experience will be as much you as at any other time.

What if we are interested in other conscious minds arising from your brain resulting from different interpretation systems, bizarre though they may be? Can you experience them first-hand? All we need is an experience producer that can translate from one interpretation system to another. That's no more of a problem than anything else we've encountered here.

Of course, from the point of view of a zombic materialist, everything is a bit simpler. They would just need to understand the brain processes that are going on and all of the physical causes and effects, and would not have to worry about the phenomenal. However, this is not to say that they would not benefit from the use of experience producers.

They would still have the same problem of having to digest complex physical data in order to understand psychological consciousness. And using the experience producer to put their own brain into certain states would help them to understand the physical data in a more intuitive and all-at-once way. The experience producer need not be relegated to playtime only.

None of this would cause embarrassment to a zombic materialist. Nothing here implies a requirement for dualism or a form of non-zombic materialism. The theory of consciousness that you take on need not affect your empirical methods in this case.

But if dualism does happen to be true (as we are taking it to be), then using exactly the same techniques as the zombic materialists would lead not only to a physical understanding, but also to an understanding of the impotent reflection that is the phenomenal realm.

Part 2
Applications

Chapter 8

The Location of Consciousness

If consciousness results from brain activity, then perhaps there is a particular part of the brain where consciousness happens. Could it be that all the processing that goes on in the rest of the brain is unconscious, and that only what passes through this specific point is conscious? The idea that there is a part of the brain where 'you' are certainly has a certain intuitive appeal to it. Daniel Dennett (1991) calls this part of the brain the Cartesian Theatre but argues against its existence.

> The brain is Headquarters, the place where the ultimate observer is, but there is no reason to believe that the brain itself has any deeper headquarters, any inner sanctum, arrival at which is the necessary or sufficient condition for conscious experiences. In short, there is no observer inside the brain.[38]

In his case against the existence of a Cartesian Theatre, Dennett argues that there is no central place where a completed brain process goes for it to become conscious; processing is continuous and doesn't pass a threshold of consciousness at any time or in any place.

But as American philosopher Arnold Zuboff (1994) argues, some parts of the brain (he uses the visual cortex as an example) only seem important in what they set up in other brain areas, presumably where he thinks consciousness happens. To illustrate his point, Zuboff uses the example of a randomly firing shell that replaces the visual cortex:

---

[38] p. 106

We should consider a case of the replacement of the visual cortex by a gadget that feeds merely random impulses into the rest of the brain. This could be just a shell with energy randomly playing on its surface and flowing into the surrounding nerves. It may seem that the result for the state of the functions in this case would be chaotic. But let's also imagine that this substitution has been tried in countless different cases, and we are now attending to a case in which the pattern in the rest of the brain ended up accidentally precisely as the normal visual cortex would have produced it.[39]

The shell does not have any of the internal workings of the visual cortex; it is effectively a hollow shell that replaces only the points of contact with the rest of the brain. But the random shell still fires so that the rest of the brain receives the same information that it would have done normally. Zuboff has suggested here that the experiment is run countless times so that one case where it fires as normal becomes a probable outcome, although thought experiments do not really need to be probable. However, some might be happier with a probable situation, and Zuboff is catering for these people.

In this example, Zuboff argues that the subject would still consciously see as normal; the job of the visual cortex has been done, even if not in the normal way, and the necessary neural states have still been set up in the rest of the brain:

> But surely the visual experience must still be phenomenologically the same as it would have been with the [...] visual cortex. The subject would speak and do the same; so it must all be seeming the same to him.[40]

However, if the entire brain is replaced by this shell, which still happens by chance to produce the same behaviour, Zuboff does not have the same view:

> I think our shell-brained creature, despite its impressive pattern of movements and sounds, precisely those of a proper person, would have no psychological state at all. The operation of this thing involves no mental functioning. With no functions there is no experience, no mind, only show.[41]

---

[39] pp. 194–195
[40] p. 195
[41] p. 195

And if just one hemisphere were replaced in this fashion:

> In the remaining normal hemisphere there would be mistaken impressions of normality in the whole, while in the shell there would really be no functions and no experience.[42]

And to summarise:

> It seems to me therefore that the shell that neatly replaced a function could be properly participating, even though only accidentally, in the set of tensions that is experience. The shell that replaced the whole brain, however, would be doing no more than accidentally matching an external pattern of movements that any number of such tensions might have produced; but this would be without the tensions, without experience.[43]

It is interesting that Zuboff argues that replacing just the visual cortex would have no effect on consciousness, rather than resulting in a certain loss of consciousness, albeit smaller than the loss from removing a whole hemisphere. It would appear that Zuboff regards some brain areas as more important than others in terms of consciousness production. Perhaps it is true that the visual cortex is not conscious itself but is only relevant in terms of setting up the conscious area. This would make it a functional element (or part of an even larger functional element), which we discussed in chapter 2. However, this is certainly not the view of Dennett (1991), who does not see the brain as having designated conscious and unconscious areas.

> [T]here is no one place in the brain through which all these causal trains must pass in order to deposit their content "in consciousness."[44]

From an evolutionary point of view, all brain areas are important only in terms of how they fit into the bigger picture, which is overall functioning. There is no part of the brain whose job it is to be conscious, even if consciousness does happen to be centred

---

[42] p. 195
[43] p. 196
[44] p. 135

there. But is it likely that there is one part of the brain where consciousness is centred? The visual cortex may seem important only in terms of what it helps to set up in other brain areas, but ultimately all brain areas are important only in terms of what they allow to happen elsewhere. There is no end point in the brain. The brain is there for its functional and, ultimately, its behavioural effects. So while the visual cortex exists only for its functional effects, it is, in that respect, like all parts of the brain. You cannot remove all the functions and expect to have a part of the brain left for experience. And it certainly does not make sense to say that you can remove any function individually without affecting consciousness, but not all of them at once, if this is Zuboff's claim. It would be as if the remaining functions could compensate for the missing function by providing the consciousness normally associated with the missing function!

The view that makes most sense to me is that by removing functions one by one (and replacing them with the random shell), you would reduce the amount of consciousness bit by bit. Looking at it this way, replacing the whole brain with a randomly firing shell eliminates all of the conscious experience, replacing one hemisphere eliminates probably about half of the consciousness, and replacing the whole visual cortex eliminates a certain proportion of the consciousness, which is likely to be roughly equivalent to the proportion of the brain's functioning that takes place there. It might be that some types of functioning produce more consciousness than other types, even if there is the same amount of functioning involved in each, so it wouldn't necessarily be just about proportion of functioning. In any case, the visual cortex seems far too large to be functionally elemental.

If we did briefly entertain the idea of a Cartesian Theatre, then how large would it be? If it is a single point (say one neuron), then we are effectively saying that we could do away with the whole rest of the brain and replace it with a tiny randomly firing shell, connected to the Cartesian-Theatre neuron, as long as it resulted in the right firings for the one neuron, and our whole consciousness would be unaffected. And what if in our normal brain that one neuron died? Would consciousness go completely? This does not seem realistic. If we say that the Theatre consists of a group of neurons, then why stop at some arbitrary number and cordon off that section of the brain? All of the brain is involved in functioning, so it seems more likely that it is all important for consciousness production. Also, as soon as we admit that the Cartesian Theatre is larger than a single point, it defeats our reasons for postulating its existence, since the idea behind it is that there is a central point in the brain where 'you' reside. If it's larger than a single point, the same reasoning would lead you to wonder where within it 'you' reside.

If it is neurons' role in the overall functional system that determines whether they are important for consciousness, then we could also look outside the brain. It is normally assumed that consciousness happens only in the brain, but other parts of the body are involved in the human functional system. There is processing of sorts going on all over the body. The most complex processing may happen in the brain, but that only indicates that the brain is responsible for most of the consciousness, not necessarily all of it. For example, before any visual data reaches the visual cortex, it is processed to an extent by the eye. And all other senses are, to some extent, processed by other parts of the body before they reach the brain. The processing is certainly not as complex as what happens in the brain, but this is only a matter of degree.

This extension of the mind can be taken even further. The environment can also be seen as part of the functional system that determines our conscious states. Dennett (1996a) gives a good example regarding the elderly:

> It is commonly observed – but not commonly enough! – that old folks removed from their homes to hospital settings are put at a tremendous disadvantage, even though their basic bodily needs are well provided for. They often *appear* to be quite demented – to be utterly incapable of feeding, clothing, and washing themselves, let alone engaging in activities of greater interest. Often, however, if they are returned to their homes, they can manage quite well for themselves. How do they do this? Over the years, they have loaded their home environments with ultrafamiliar landmarks, triggers for habits, reminders of what to do [...] Taking them out of their homes is literally separating them from large parts of their minds –

potentially just as devastating a development as undergoing brain surgery.[45]

The landmarks in their homes are part of their overall functional system. The brain and environment both contain certain reference points that enable us to function properly. The only difference is that the environmental reference points are outside the body. Why should the location – being inside or outside the brain – make a difference to whether consciousness is produced as a result?

Intuitively, it seems that the environment can be done away with without affecting our consciousness. If you had a brain in a vat, which had the correct inputs and outputs, so that there was no real outside world but just the perception of it, most people would probably accept that this brain had normal consciousness. But obviously in this case, the rest of the environment (including the non-brain part of the body) would still be functionally represented by this system. However, if the inputs into the brain representing the environment were randomised (as long as, by chance, they were the same as they would be for a normal environment), I think most people would still intuitively say that no consciousness would be lost. After all, the brain – the seemingly important organ for consciousness – is still intact.

The brain certainly seems to form a larger proportion of the relevant functional system than the environment – it is physically smaller but more of the functioning is done there. But does that make the environment dispensable? If it does, then that seems to be the same as dispensing with an equivalently sized (in functional terms) part of the brain and replacing that with a randomly firing shell (that happens to result in the rest of the brain firing as normal). And if this has no effect on consciousness, then we could replace more and more of the brain, bit by bit, with the randomly firing shell, until there was no brain left. You could reach a point where all that is left is random firings representing just the parts of the brain in direct contact with the rest of the body – just enough to keep the behaviour of the person as normal. But since we would not accept this person as having a proper conscious mind, it seems that we have

---

[45] pp. 138–139, italics in original

to accept at least the possibility that the environment is a factor in determining consciousness. We certainly haven't ruled it out yet. However, as mentioned previously, it is not necessarily just about the amount of functioning, but possibly also about the type of functioning. But I see no particular reason to suggest that the type of functioning that takes place inside the brain holds a monopoly in what it takes to produce consciousness. This is at least something worthy of consideration.

In Dennett's example with the elderly, there is certainly relevant functioning involving the environment. The fact that it is outside the human body doesn't change anything regarding its functional importance. A functionalist theory of consciousness considers only the function and does not discriminate on the basis of geography (I discuss this point again in chapter 12). Indeed, we can imagine a brain in a vat where some of the brain's functioning is outsourced to silicon chips in an off-site location, but still in contact by radio communication.

The idea that the brain produces all of our consciousness is certainly intuitive, but this alone does not make it correct. If the brain is an important determining factor for consciousness, then it seems that the environment is likely to be too. This means that some consciousness could be lost if the environment were randomised in the brain-in-a-vat example above. But as I have said, the brain does form a larger proportion of the relevant functional system – immensely so – so it is important to emphasise that having a random environment could only make a negligible difference to the consciousness.

The idea that consciousness is altered simply by randomising the environment while the brain remains unchanged is intuitively absurd, but if we ignore that possibility, the shell within the brain causes us a bigger headache. If this is a problem, it is a problem for a functional theory of consciousness. But this is the best choice we have without resorting to zombic materialism and giving up on consciousness altogether.

It is possible that some parts of the brain are more important in creating consciousness than other parts of equal physical size, so that replacing some parts of the brain with random shells would cause a bigger loss of consciousness than with other parts. Using Zuboff's example again, it could perhaps be that the visual cortex is one of the less important parts. This could also lead one to the conclusion that there is a part of the brain that has the most importance in the production of consciousness (perhaps the part with the highest 'consciousness per neuron' or 'consciousness per unit volume' ratio), and this could be seen as a Cartesian Theatre of sorts. However, it would only be one in a loose sense, since it would be the most conscious part, rather than the only conscious part.

Dennett's assertion that '[t]he brain is Headquarters [...] but there is no reason to believe that the brain itself has any deeper head-quarters' seems to be a little simplistic. Indeed, his own example with the elderly seems to indicate this. Functioning does not begin and end with the brain, and even within the brain, some parts have more complex functioning than others.

Andy Clark and David Chalmers (1998) argue the case for the mind extending into the environment, but not the conscious part of the mind:

> Some find this sort of externalism unpalatable. One reason may be that many identify the cognitive with the conscious, and it seems far from plausible that consciousness extends outside the head in these cases. But not every cognitive process, at least on standard usage, is a conscious process. It is widely accepted that all sorts of processes beyond the borders of consciousness play a crucial role in cognitive processing: in the retrieval of memories, linguistic processes, and skill acquisition, for example. So the mere fact that external processes are external where consciousness is internal is no reason to deny that those processes are cognitive.[46]

It is an interesting point that they raise, but if you disregard the possibility that consciousness extends outside the brain, arguing how far the non-conscious mind extends is largely a matter of defi-nitions. As discussed in chapter 7 regarding the views of Dennett, mere psychological consciousness comes down to how you define it. In any case, I do not see it as implausible that environmental func-tioning can cause consciousness any more than I see it as

---

[46] p. 10

implausible that a 'hunk of gray matter' (to borrow from Chalmers himself (1996, p. 251)) can, even if the environment only plays a very small role.

Clark (2008) continues the line of thought into a whole book on the extended mind, which is very interesting in its own right, but it is still concerned with the non-conscious mind.

Talking of these functional parts of the environment contributing to consciousness is not too far removed from the ideas involved in panpsychism, where everything has a certain amount of conscious-ness. We are talking about external subsystems of very limited functional complexity, possibly in some cases as limited as that of a thermostat, adding to the consciousness of a functionally larger system. This may seem unreasonable, but you could likewise break the brain down into arbitrarily small parts, where each of these parts is no more complex than a thermostat. This does not imply panpsy-chism, however, as it may be possible that such a limited device can add to the consciousness of a larger system of which it is a part, without necessarily having any consciousness when considered on its own. I am not too bothered by the possibility of these subsystems having a (very) limited form of consciousness when considered alone, and do not feel the need to draw a conclusion on this, as I also discussed in chapter 4. As I have stated previously, type of function-ing rather than just complexity may be a factor, so the functioning of the environment may simply not be of the right type to produce consciousness, which could also stop thermostats from being conscious. But I have seen no reason to simply write off the possibil-ity, since we are far from sure what the 'right type' of functioning looks like.

Philosopher Alva Noë (2009) argues that consciousness is not simply produced by the brain, but produced by the interaction between the brain, the body and the environment. His view is arguably a more extreme form of the extended mind theory. He argues that brain-in-a-vat thought experiments do not do justice to the role the environment plays:

> My own view is that the suggestion that cells in a dish could be conscious – or that you could have a conscious brain in a vat – is absurd [...] The vat would have to be very complicated and special-

ized in order to control the administration of stimulation to the brain comparable to that normally provided to a brain by its environmentally situated body. If you actually try to think through the details of this thought experiment – this is something scientists and philosophers struck by the brain-in-a-vat idea almost never do – it's clear that the vat would have to be, in effect, something like a living body. [...] Maybe consciousness depends on reliable interactions between what is going on in the brain and what is going on in nonbrain parts of the body. It could even turn out that consciousness depends on interactions between the brain and the body and bits of the world nearby. So maybe, to get consciousness in the dish, we'd need not only brain and body but also a reasonable facsimile of the environment in the dish too.[47]

I have already indirectly addressed this point, but it's best to spell it out. A simulation of the environment is needed for the brain in a vat to receive the right inputs to continue to function as normal, and for consciousness to do so as well. However, this is not to say that the environment is where the consciousness is produced. If, as discussed, the brain in a vat received random stimulation so that the inputs happened to match what would be received from a realistic environment, we would expect consciousness to continue as before, with at most a negligible loss. However, if we did the opposite and stimulated the environment with random inputs that happened to represent what a human being might do, we would not expect any more than a negligible consciousness to be produced, if any at all. Regardless of where one stands on whether the body outside the brain or the environment contribute to the production of consciousness, their contribution in terms of actual amount of consciousness production is at most negligible.

The conclusion from this chapter is that while there is no one place in the brain responsible for consciousness production and no Cartesian Theatre, some parts of the brain may still play a larger role than others. The rest of the body and even the environment possibly play a role as well, however minor that role is.

---

[47] pp. 12–13

Chapter 9

Unity of Consciousness

Processing is going on all over our brains and there is no centre of consciousness in the brain, but there still seems to be some sort of unity to it all. Presumably, you think that you are one self with one mind, and while you may have different thoughts at a given time, they are all unified (not necessarily in terms of a place, as discussed, but at least consciously), and there is just one keeper of these thoughts. Is this really how it is or is it just an illusion?

The idea that there might not be unity to consciousness in some people is highlighted in patients who have had their corpus callosum (a connection between the two hemispheres of the brain) severed, in a procedure known as 'commissurotomy'. This severe act used to be a standard treatment for epilepsy to 'quarantine' the seizure in one hemisphere. Michael Gazzaniga and Joseph LeDoux (1978) discussed the implications of this procedure in great detail.

While these patients appear to function fairly normally most of the time, certain tests show that each hemisphere of the brain often doesn't know what the other one is doing. If, for example, the patients are shown objects to just the left half of their visual field, then only their right hemisphere will be aware of the object (the left visual field is linked with the right hemisphere and vice versa). They will not verbally report seeing the object (language is normally generated in the left hemisphere), and they will be able to pick out the object later on only with their left hand (controlled by the right hemisphere).

Of course, these patients are not normal subjects, so their behaviour may not appear to be a problem for most people's consciousness unity. However, in one experiment reported by Gazzaniga and LeDoux (pp. 14–15; originally in Risse &

Gazzaniga, 1976), the unity of even normal subjects was brought into question.

The left hemispheres of these normal subjects were put to sleep, effectively putting the right side of the body to sleep. An object was then placed in their left hand (controlled by the awake right hemisphere). Later, when the subjects were fully awake, they could not identify the object when asked, and displayed no verbal signs of any knowledge of its existence (language being controlled by the left hemisphere). But when several objects were placed in front of the subject, they could point at the correct object with their left hand (the hand the object was earlier placed in). Even after fully awakening, only their right hemisphere had the information, which seems to show that there was not complete unity in these subjects even after their brains were back to normal. It would appear that these subjects did in some sense consciously know which was the correct object, so apparently even in normal subjects one hemisphere can have conscious information not accessible to the other hemisphere. This may not be a normal situation, but once the anaesthetic had worn off, these subjects' consciousness should have been as unified as anyone else's.

As Dennett (1991) argues, split-brain patients do not simply split into two selves because:

> it *isn't* the case that commissurotomy leaves in its wake organisations both distinct and robust enough to support such a separate self.[48]

Also, there is still information flow between the hemispheres, but it has been reduced by a matter of degree:

> This leaves the hemispheres still indirectly connected, through a variety of midbrain structures.[49]

It is an oversimplification to say that each normal brain has exactly one consciousness, which has complete unity, and that if the corpus callosum is severed, then there are exactly two well-defined consciousnesses. In normal brains, each hemisphere does not have

---

[48] p. 426, italics in original
[49] p. 423

access to everything in the other hemisphere, and in split-brain patients each hemisphere does still have access to some information in the other hemisphere. Unity of consciousness is about connectedness between areas of the brain and would, therefore, appear to come in degrees rather than as an all-or-nothing affair. Perhaps it would make more sense to talk about degrees of connectedness of consciousness rather than unity, as unity seems to imply an absolute with no degrees.

Your 'verbal' consciousness is not aware of how you display all the skills that you possess, even if they are performed consciously in some sense. To explain in words how to perform a specific physical task (such as driving, or typing on a keyboard), you may have to watch yourself performing the task, or visualise yourself doing so, before your verbal consciousness can gain access to this knowledge. But you would still call the actions conscious. It is not simply about some people having unity to their consciousness and some not. No-one's consciousness is fully unified.

Due to the lack of unity, some brain processing that is considered to be unconscious (or subconscious) may not actually be unconscious, but just not strongly connected to the parts of the brain responsible for speech, so it cannot readily be talked about. This may lead you to the conclusion that if it is conscious then it has a separate consciousness, but it is not that simple, as you may have gathered by now. Weakly connected does not mean not connected at all. There may be some intermediate brain processing which is fairly strongly connected to both parts of the brain, so which of the two supposedly separate consciousnesses would this lie in? It is impossible to draw distinct lines between different parts of the brain and say that they have separate minds, simply because they are not distinct from each other. How well connected different parts of the brain are is just a matter of degree.

Blindsight is an interesting phenomenon, and it is often brought up by academics in books and articles on consciousness, e.g. Dennett (1991, pp. 322–333), so it is worth briefly discussing it here. Each part of the visual field corresponds to a certain area of the primary visual cortex in the brain. And when people suffer damage to their primary visual cortex, they become blind in the part of their visual field corresponding to that part of the primary visual cortex. But in some cases, when objects are placed in that part of their visual field, they can perform at above-chance levels in determining what is happening in their blind area by 'guessing'. What is going on here? There are other, more primitive, parts of the brain that still process the visual information that the primary visual cortex now cannot. The processing is less complex than that of the primary visual cortex, so likely to be less conscious. But this is not to say that it is entirely unconscious. Information still flows from these parts of the brain to the parts of the brain involved in speech and behaviour, but since the information flow is not great, the subject does not necessarily notice it and it is deemed unconscious. But the difference between this and a 'normal' conscious flow is one of degree, not type. The subject may think that they are making a complete guess at what is in their visual field, when really there are certain cues that they are not strongly aware of that are influencing their behaviour.

Blindsight and split-brains, along with many other brain disorders, are popular subject matter for philosophers. And they are important tools for helping us to understand human consciousness. However, in terms of finding a general theory relating matter and consciousness (as opposed to just human consciousness), they are less important, since we could imagine a being with any brain disorder we liked, as long as it is logically possible. Feel free to make up your own. The fact that a disorder has not been seen in humans does not make it any less relevant to a complete theory relating matter and consciousness. Of course, such disorders in humans have still helped to guide our thinking in certain directions, which can help us in our quest for a general theory. But now that we have been trained to think along these lines, the discovery of any new brain disorder would probably not have very much philosophical significance.

Drawing on the previous chapter, if two different parts of the brain are considered to be of equal size in functional terms (or at least in consciousness-producing terms), it might seem that replacing one with a randomly firing shell (by chance leaving the rest of the brain functioning as normal) would have the same effect as replacing the other in the same manner. However, while these replacements may result in a loss of the same amount of consciousness, this does not necessarily mean that their effect is identical. Eliminating different parts of the brain in this way further brings into question the unity of consciousness. The brain performs a lot of different functions, and replacing one functional area with a randomly firing shell could mean that a specific part of the consciousness is eliminated rather than simply a proportion of the consciousness removed globally.

Furthermore, this discussion is not just about parts of the brain and their connectedness. It is about the whole functional system, which, as discussed, arguably extends beyond the brain into the rest of the body, and even into the environment beyond.

But what is the whole functional system? The entire universe could be seen as a single functional system. After all, your body and brain are just one part of the universe, and it could be considered to be an arbitrary move to draw lines marking out separate individuals. All minds could be linked, so perhaps it could even be argued that there is only one mind. But this doesn't seem right. Even if all the consciousness in the universe were linked together in some way, it wouldn't all be connected very strongly or equally. I'm sure that you don't consider all the consciousness in the universe to be of equal relevance in terms of your consciousness. Saying that there is just one mind just doesn't seem to fit the data. On the other hand, we arguably cannot really separate all the consciousness out into distinct minds. An alternative to these ideas, however, is overlapping minds.

As discussed in the previous chapter, the environmental functioning may not be conscious anyway, avoiding many of these problems, but it's worth discussing this topic, to allow for a more complete coverage of the possibilities. This is also a very speculative idea.

So to continue with the concept of overlapping minds, in this case, each part of the functioning in the universe would be the centre of consciousness for a particular self, but each self would not be completely sealed off from all others. So one part of the functioning would be at the centre of one self, and there would be other parts of the functioning that would only be experienced weakly by this self, as they would only be a peripheral part of this self. For example, there would be a conscious self (Self A) whose centre is in the area of the brain responsible for creating speech, and there would be another part of the brain whose processing might be considered unconscious by Self A because the connection is not strong enough between the two parts.

However, there would also be a Self B for which that peripheral part of Self A would be the central point, and the strongly experienced parts of Self A would only be experienced weakly by Self B. So Self A's so-called unconscious processing would actually be the central point for this particular conscious self. Both these selves would contain the same conscious content, but in differing strengths, or levels of access. Effectively each human brain would have many different selves, with different areas of the brain being the central point for different selves. Of course, many of these minds would be very similar to each other, as you could shift the central point fractionally and still get a slightly different self. This central point would be another possible use for the term 'Cartesian Theatre', but again only in a loose sense, as it is not the meaning that was originally intended. This 'many minds per brain' idea is, of course, completely separate from that discussed in chapter 6 involving multiple interpretations of a brain state.

And as with the idea discussed in chapter 6, it is probably not worth worrying too much about these alternative minds. You could narrow down the 'relevant' minds to the ones centralised in parts of the brain where the higher-level reportable processing happens and where there is a sense of self.

Regarding the idea that environmental functioning connects all minds together: while there may be functioning of sorts in the environment, it would be negligible compared to that of human brains, so there would effectively be a functional void between each pair of brains, and each brain could quite reasonably be considered as a separate unit. Also, while any sort of communication between two people would strengthen the link between their brains by increasing the flow of information, it would still be negligible compared to the flow of information within one brain, so still not worth worrying about.

A possible real-life case of overlapping minds is conjoined twins

Krista and Tatiana Hogan. Their brains are connected, and while they each have their own personalities, there is evidence that they can share what each other experiences, although not in a fully unified manner. For example, when Krista consumed some ketchup, which she likes, Tatiana, who dislikes ketchup, made an expression of disgust. See Hirstein (2012).

According to Giulio Tononi's information integration theory of consciousness (e.g. 2007), the amount of consciousness that a system has is determined by the amount of information that it can integrate, and he calls this measure Φ (the Greek letter, pronounced 'phi'). He also argues that the brain is not just one conscious system but has many complexes, each with their own value of Φ.

> [W]e calculate Φ for every possible subset of a system, and discard all those subsets that are included in larger subsets having higher Φ (being merely parts of a larger whole). What we are left with is *complexes* – individual entities that can integrate information.[50]

Tononi is saying that if two systems were not very well connected so that the combined system would have a lower level of Φ than each of the two systems considered separately, then this combined system would not be considered a conscious mind. On the other hand, if the combined system were well enough connected to have a larger value of Φ than each of the two smaller systems individually, then the smaller systems would not be individually conscious, but just part of a larger consciousness. However, this still does not neatly partition the brain, or physical existence generally, into separate conscious units, because:

> [T]he same element can belong to more than one complex, and complexes can overlap.[51]

This may end up with a slightly neater state of affairs than what I have just proposed, but there would still be overlapping minds, and I'm not sure it is necessarily more realistic as a theory, as it seems to be a fairly arbitrary means of discounting possible minds. That's not

---

[50] p. 292, italics in original
[51] p. 292

to say that there's no value in Φ as a measure of consciousness, and indeed I will return to the idea in the final chapter.

The idea of overlapping minds in one brain is unlikely to sit well with Daniel Dennett. According to his 'fame in the brain' theory (e.g. 2005, pp. 136–143), a thought is only conscious once it has taken hold and 'reverberates' around the brain, and if it fails to reach this level, then it fails to reach consciousness. So it would not be simply that brain functions each get to be a centre of consciousness in their own right, as I am suggesting, but that a brain function has to make itself known throughout the brain for it to become conscious at all. This is an interesting point, but I see this reverberation as certain functions connecting up to form a stronger consciousness than if they were going it alone, rather than connecting up to form a consciousness that would not have existed at all otherwise. Consciousness comes in degrees, not as an all-or-nothing affair. Fame in the brain simply implies a greater strength of consciousness. After all, something that failed to reach the fame threshold may still be consciously retrievable at a later date, given the right interrogation, as shown by another example from Dennett (1991):

> Are you constantly conscious of the clock ticking? If it suddenly stops, you notice this, and you can say right away what it is that has stopped; the ticks "you weren't conscious of" up to the moment they stopped and "would never have been conscious of" if they hadn't stopped are now clearly in your consciousness. An even more striking case is the phenomenon of being able to count, retrospectively in experience memory, the chimes of the clock which you only noticed was striking after four or five chimes. But how could you so clearly *remember hearing* something you hadn't been conscious of in the first place? The question betrays a commitment to the Cartesian model; there are no fixed facts about the stream of consciousness independent of particular probes.[52]

According to this passage, it is not a simple fact whether the chimes were in your consciousness before you noticed them. Since his later work seems to imply that he would now say that they were not in your consciousness until they reached 'fame' status, I will take that as

---

[52] pp. 137–138, italics in original

Dennett's view, and disagree with it. I think that you certainly would be conscious of the 'unnoticed' chimes, but if the thought didn't reverberate and never reached 'fame', then it would only be a weak conscious thought, involving a small amount of functioning, and only peripheral to the parts of consciousness related to behaviour.

Another interesting point is change blindness (e.g. Dennett, 2005, pp. 82–91). This is where someone is shown two alternating pictures that are virtually identical, but have one difference. The different images can flip before your eyes without you noticing the difference, but once you are alerted to the difference, it is quite clear. Before you notice the change, are your conscious experiences of the two images different? Dennett uses this example to show how people who use the term 'qualia' often do not really know what they mean by it. But regardless of whether one uses the term 'qualia', I would argue that there is a change in conscious experience when the images flip. Once the change is noticed, it may have more 'fame in the brain', but this is a matter of degree. As I argued in chapter 1, you can never be conscious of all of your consciousness, so you cannot be expected to notice every change in experience. The change in conscious experience would be there, but would have no strong connection to the parts of your consciousness that are related to speech and behaviour.

Dennett (1991) is quite explicit that his theory of consciousness:

> brusquely denies the possibility in principle of consciousness of a stimulus in the absence of the subject's belief in that consciousness.[53]

I would disagree with this for the reasons above.

All that has been said so far assumes that there is some degree of connectedness to our consciousness, and that different parts of the brain, and therefore consciousness, have differing strengths of connectedness between them. But now I am going to look at the possibility that there is no connectedness to consciousness at all, and that it is just an illusion.

I am going to reuse Zuboff's (1994) randomly-firing-shell thought experiment (discussed in the previous chapter) for a different purpose. Imagine that one hemisphere of a brain is taken

---

[53] p. 132

away altogether and replaced with a randomly firing shell, which, as before, happens to result in the remaining hemisphere firing as it would have done if the other hemisphere had not been replaced.

By doing this we would be keeping one half of the brain functioning as normal and basically doing away with the rest. As we concluded previously, it would seem that we would have lost a lot of the consciousness (presumably about half of it), because we would only have half the brain. But the remaining hemisphere would be unaffected, and would certainly be under the impression that there was a full and normal conscious experience even if there were not. It would be functioning as normal, so there would be no room for the realisation that half the consciousness is missing to creep in. So the consciousness that did exist would think that there was more consciousness than there really was. It seems that we would have half a consciousness that thought it was whole.

This can be taken further by removing more and more of the brain. We could have a quarter of the brain surrounded by a randomly firing shell, which, by chance, results in the normal functioning of the quarter of the brain that remains. The consciousness created by that quarter of a brain would think that it had the full consciousness of a whole brain, or it certainly would not be aware that anything was missing, at least. We could take this as far as we want. But there would come a point where it would seem absurd to suggest that such a small part of a brain could think that it had the consciousness of a whole brain. If there were one neuron left, which was firing as that one neuron would in a normal brain, would that create the illusion of a full consciousness?

Of course it could not. The consciousness that remained at any point along this line would simply be the same as it was in that part of the brain before. So only in a part of the brain large enough to be capable of thinking about consciousness would the illusion exist.

It should be pointed out that while each unaffected part of the brain might contain the same consciousness as it would have had the shell not replaced the rest of the brain, this is not the same as saying that a self that is centred in that part of the brain would be unaffected. If we are still entertaining the idea of selves stretching across several brain areas and beyond, the peripheral parts of this self would still be affected by the shell taking over. You would just not be aware of it.

Going back to the real world, while we can be fairly certain that we haven't had parts of our brains replaced with a randomly firing shell, this could still have further implications to do with the unity or connectedness of consciousness in real brains.

The brain could be split into many separate consciousnesses as a matter of course, and the connectedness between them might be just an illusion. It is clear from the above that you would not notice if this were the case. This connectedness could be seen as an extra layer of complexity and against Ockham's Razor, since it seems we could do away with it without anyone noticing. There might be no connectedness to consciousness at all even within a brain, let alone across the whole universe as one big functional system.

But we shouldn't get too carried away. I would argue that the idea of there being no connectedness to consciousness at all does not seem to be the most realistic scenario. It writes off the idea of there being consciousness of any complexity at all, and we might as well embrace zombic materialism, since what we would be left with would be not far away from it, if we took it to its logical conclusions. We left zombic materialism behind because we wanted to see what things follow from the existence of the consciousness that we perceive to exist. The no-connectedness-to-consciousness idea is not the consciousness that we perceive to exist, or even close, and in an Ockham's Razor battle against zombic materialism, it would lose horribly.

I am also not sure that it makes sense to have a consciousness with no connectedness, so any argument against the connectedness of consciousness could be seen as an argument for zombic materialism. For there to be any sort of functional state, there would presumably need to be at least some form of interaction and, therefore, connectedness. With just one rigid part to the system, I can't see consciousness having anywhere to exist, unless it is intrinsic to particles. So while I would still perhaps consider the view to be a remote possibility, there is really nowhere else to go with it and it will not be further pursued. The idea was really to see where the thought experiment ended up, and it has now been exhausted.

Likewise, the idea that there could ever be full unity to consciousness does not seem plausible. If a conscious entity has more than just one rigid part, then there will always be a reliance on imperfect connections between functional parts. Full unity implies that all the information in a conscious part of the brain is constantly ready for instant retrieval by any other conscious part of the brain.

It is intuitive for us to think that we have a unified consciousness, presumably because it has been evolutionarily hardwired into us. However, we could easily imagine a being that was hardwired into thinking that its consciousness was not unified, despite having the same level of connectedness as our own consciousness. We can be wrong about our consciousness. There is also no psychological or physical counterpart to phenomenal unity. Our brains are not fully unified, as I have just argued, and so consciousness cannot be either, unless it has properties that are unrelated to the physical world. To borrow from Dennett again, it would be epiphenomenal gremlins gone mad.

In conclusion, it is clearly not the case that each brain has exactly one consciousness, with full unity, and that is completely separate from any other consciousness. Where there is doubt is the exact degree of connectedness between different conscious experiences across the brain, body, outside environment, and indeed the whole universe. The overlapping selves theory is certainly worthy of consideration. There would still be fairly definite cut-off points, since there would effectively be a functional vacuum between each pair of brains. Each self would have a central point, but it would not be a true Cartesian Theatre since there would be peripheral conscious experience as well. There can never be a true Cartesian Theatre since consciousness always requires multiple parts of a functional system.

Chapter 10

Personal Identity

I have discussed various problems of consciousness throughout this book. But who is it that experiences the consciousness? Most people would probably think of themselves as a continually existing self through time. For each physical human there seems to be a single conscious self throughout the human's life. Before that human existed, that self never existed, and after they die, that self will never exist again. But during the human's life, while there will be different conscious experiences, it will still be the same conscious entity, or self, experiencing them. Is this the correct view? Does each physical body have a single self throughout its life? Are you the same self that existed five, or ten, years ago? To answer these questions, we need to determine what the defining properties of a self are, and I am going to use some thought experiments to help us do this.

Thought Experiments

You agree to take part in an experiment that involves spending the night in a laboratory. There are 100 beds in the room, and you sleep in the one bed that has 'master' written on it. The other 99 empty beds are labelled 'copy' and numbered 1 to 99 respectively. While you are asleep, at some particular point in the night, some scientists take a scan of your whole body including your brain. The scientists use the scan of you to create 99 identical copies of you and these are placed in beds 1 to 99, all while you are still asleep. You are told all this in advance. You agree to this experiment because you are being paid, and because you can go home in the morning without anything having been done to you, apart from a non-invasive scan. Seems OK, doesn't it? But when you wake up in the morning, a thought suddenly hits you that makes you too scared to open your eyes.

When you went to sleep, you expected to wake up in the master bed, as that is where you went to sleep, and to leave the laboratory with more money than when you went in. But there are 99 other people all waking up with exactly the same thoughts as you, as they are identical, or were as recently as last night. What extra knowledge do you now have that they don't, which proves that you are the real you? On the other hand, you went to sleep as you, and have now surely woken up as you. These other people have been created completely separately from you. You would be sure who you were if they had not been created, so why should that change now? They have not come into contact with you or contaminated you in any way. You went to sleep and woke up as usual. So should you be confident of waking up in the master bed or have you only got a 1% chance?

The point is that there are 100 people, including you, going through exactly the same thought processes, and none of them have any knowledge which allows them to confidently separate themselves out as the true you until they open their eyes and see which bed they are in. The fact that they haven't physically contaminated you is irrelevant. And even then, one of the scientists might have swapped people round from bed to bed as a trick! But let's not further complicate matters. From the knowledge you have now, before you open your eyes, there is a 99% chance that you are a copy that was created in the night.

What conclusions can we draw from this thought experiment? It shows that someone can be convinced that they have existed in the past when in reality they haven't. The idea that you are a continuously existing self is created by your memories and does not necessarily reflect how it really is. So perhaps it could be that the self doesn't survive any longer than a moment in time, and each change creates a new self. How could we know otherwise? Or perhaps it shows that anyone with your memories can rightly claim to be you. Back to the thought experiment ...

Here's a further twist. You go to sleep in the laboratory, and the scientists take a scan of you as in the previous example, but this time they do nothing with it immediately. Before you go to sleep, you are told that they are going to hold onto the data until one night, 100 years in the future, when they are going to create 99 copies identical to how you were when they took the scan. You wake up in the morning thinking that you must be the real you because the other copies haven't been brought into existence yet. But is this confidence really justified? You suddenly realise that you only think that it is the next morning because of what is in your memory. The 99 copies will all wake up in 100 years' time thinking exactly the same as you. They will also think that they must be the real you because it is the morning after the scan has been taken, and the copies haven't been created yet, so there is no chance that *they* are a copy. But they are all wrong.

Again, in this example, you have no knowledge that allows you to confidently state that you are the original you. This may be more counterintuitive than the last example, but all 100 people, including you, will be thinking exactly the same things upon waking, and nothing in those thoughts is enough to prove anyone's identity. You still only have a 1% chance of being 'you'.

This example leaves us with a further complication. You might not be completely sure that the scientists are actually going to produce the copies in the future, even if they assure you that they will. Anything could happen within the next 100 years to stop the scientists from completing the experiment. If you do wake up as you, apparently against all the odds, should you take that as evidence that they will ultimately fail to do so? Have you just seen into the future or have you just been very lucky? The idea that you can use this as evidence of what the scientists will do in the future seems paradoxical, because surely what may or may not happen in the future cannot have any bearing on the here and now. Otherwise there seems to have been some form of informational time travel. I will to return to this point because I am not in a position to resolve it here. But for now, let's start again with another scenario.

One night, 1,000 years ago, a super-being made some predictions about the future. And they've all been right so far. Among these predictions was the exact state of your body at a point tonight when you are asleep. In order to make this prediction, he must have correctly predicted your existence, so it seems likely he'll get this right too. According to the stories, that night, 1,000 years ago, the super-being made 99 copies identical to how you are going to be at that point tonight. Before you go to bed, you are told about this prediction and about the copies that the super-being made all those years ago, and you believe it. As you go to sleep, you are not worried about it, because it all happened a long time ago, and it could have no bearing on you. You wake up having not even considered any ramifications of the super-being's experiment. But when you wake up, before you open your eyes, it suddenly hits you. How do you know that it is 'now' and not 1,000 years ago? Obviously you can't have gone back in time, but how do you know that you ever existed in what you think of as the present? All you have are your current thoughts and memories, which are exactly the same as the thoughts and memories of the 99 copies that the super-being made. It dawns on you that you have a 99% chance of waking up 1,000 years in the 'past'!

You could run an experiment that is the same as one of those above, except that you (the original physical you) are called back, and the experiment is repeated several times. You may have fears that you are going to wake up as one of the copies in the first experiment and maybe a couple after that, but after you have been through the procedure ten times, you might feel more confident, and decide that your fears were misplaced. You might think that you had made a mistake when you thought you had reason to be worried, and you might go into the eleventh trial without any fear. All 100 of 'you' may wake up confident of being in the master bed, but 99 are in for a big shock.

Of course, none of this would mean anything from a third-person perspective. Before the experiment, your family might tell you that everything was alright, and then when the experiment was over, they would go up to the original you and say that they knew that there was nothing to worry about. Of course, from their point of view there was nothing to worry about. They don't need to worry about the multiplication of selves that is a source of torment for you and all of your copies. On each occasion, they get the original you back without worrying about whether they are the real you – unless the scientists start mixing people up, but, as said, that is another problem entirely. The whole thing would also mean nothing to Prarnt, our objective robot friend from chapter 5.

Thoughts on the Thought Experiments

What conclusions should we draw from all of this? Maybe 99% of the people in these examples are simply wrong about their personal identity, or maybe the self is not confined and defined by a specific physical body, and each has as much claim as each of the others to being the original self. Only one has the original body, but since the self is linked to consciousness, which we have established is not physical, maybe physical bodies do not define selves. But this is not just about physical bodies, but also about time. These thought experiments have involved people believing that they have gone forwards and even backwards in time. Perhaps even they have as much claim to being the same self as the original, despite living a long time in the past or future. What properties could define the self? Let's see where the philosophy takes us with the various possibilities.

Perhaps there could be something non-physical that stays with our physical bodies throughout our lives; an epiphenomenal consciousness would be non-physical, so there could be room for a theory of selfhood relating to this. Or there could be something that remains constant in our physical make-up throughout our lives that is required for our continued selfhood, such as particular molecules making up our brain. It could also be that there is no one specific thing that needs to stay constant, but that the important factor is gradual and continuous change, rather than sudden changes, so that you couldn't simply replace one brain with a different one and call it the same self, but if the first brain gradually changed into the second one over time then they would be the same self.

Which of these potential candidates for the defining properties of a self hold up to scrutiny? If something constant in the physical make-up of a human is important, it is difficult to see what it would be. The physical make-up of humans changes over time, and most, if not all, molecules are eventually replaced. So if there is a self that survives throughout a person's life, then the particular matter making up the person cannot be important. Of course, the possibility would still exist that physical matter is important and that new selves simply emerge over time.

What about something specific in the way the brain is arranged, such as specific neural patterns, as opposed to specific matter? This also changes with time anyway, and unless we are talking about no change in the arrangement being allowed, there would have to be an arbitrary cut-off line where if the change goes beyond that amount, a new self emerges.

In chapter 6, I concluded that consciousness is the realisation of a possible interpretation of a brain state. Consciousness itself is non-physical and only dependent on the right pattern in the physical state. The interpretation is not dependent on the specific physical matter involved. The specific matter must, therefore, be unimportant. So if there were two identical brains, they would not merely have identical minds, but they would have the same mind (or minds), because the interpretation would be the same one, even though the matter would 'only' be identical. Any theory that says that personal identity is dependent on specific physical matter falls at this point. This would also refute the theory that there is a specific epiphenomenal mind unique to each brain throughout its life. The epiphenomenal minds are not specific to physical brains but to the relevant patterns. Two identical brains, regardless of separation in space or time, would have the same epiphenomenal mind, with no difference of identity.

Does continuous existence play a role in defining the self? Can we say that a self remains the same self if the conscious mind exists continuously and any changes happen gradually rather than in sudden jumps? If so, then a brain could ultimately turn into any other brain through gradual changes, and so a mind could turn into any other mind. By gradual changes you could turn your brain into Albert Einstein's brain, and, if you really wanted, using the original molecules. As discussed, however, the original molecules would not actually be important. Which self would now exist? Yours, or Einstein's, or perhaps both? The continuous-self theory would say that it is your self that now exists, not Einstein's. However, the idea that the past is important in determining the self is similar to the dualism based on history mentioned when discussing Swampman in chapter 6. The brain that has gradually turned into a physical isomorph of Einstein's brain is physically identical to Einstein's and has exactly the same conscious experiences, so it would seem absurd to say that there is something fundamentally different about it in terms of selfhood.

If a mind keeps the same self by gradual changes, then it can take on any form by doing this, so it seems to lead to the conclusion that all minds are just one self. This is the view of Zuboff (1990), and he calls it 'universalism'. This is compatible with both the view that the new brain has your mind and the view that it has Einstein's, since you were both the same self to begin with!

At the other extreme to universalism is the view that any change in conscious experience is a change in self: that there are no selves above and beyond each specific conscious experience.

It may seem obvious to you that you are the same individual that existed a few minutes ago. You have clear and strong memories of what you have just been doing and thinking. However, memories are created by a physical system rather than by looking directly into the past, and do not necessarily have to represent the true state of affairs. Think back to the thought experiments at the start of this chapter where there are people created overnight, whose physical bodies have no past.

Obviously these people were created using an already-existing person as a template, so their consciousness does in some sense have a past, but we can easily change things. If a fully functional human, with memories of non-existent events, were created in an instant, perhaps in a similar style to Swampman, but without replacing an existing human, then they would claim to have done all sorts of things that had never happened to anyone, let alone them, and their memories would be just as strong as anyone else's. The point here is that you cannot infer from your current consciousness whether you have existed in the past with different thoughts. All you have as evidence is your own current conscious experience, which is consistent with both the view that there is a continuous self and the view that each self is simply defined by a specific conscious experience.

This reminds me of a remark made by philosopher Ludwig Wittgenstein that I found quoted by Richard Dawkins in *The God Delusion* (2006):

> 'Tell me,' the great twentieth-century philosopher Ludwig Wittgenstein once asked a friend, 'why do people always say it was natural for man to assume that the sun went round the Earth rather than that the Earth was rotating?' His friend replied, 'Well, obviously because it just *looks* as though the Sun is going round the Earth.' Wittgenstein responded, 'Well, what would it have looked like if it had looked as though the Earth was rotating?'[54]

The possibility of a continuous self seems to lead to the conclusion that there is just one self. And if there isn't a continuous self, then we are left with each experience as a separate self with nothing tying them together. These now seem to be the two most plausible views, albeit at opposite extremes, as they are the only ones without arbitrary cut-off lines.

Imagine if you swapped places with somebody else, say former Formula One racing driver Damon Hill. Physically, nothing is swapped; only your selves are swapped. All the thoughts and memories stay with the brain that has physically encoded them. 'You' would become Damon Hill and carry on leading his life unaware that you had ever been anyone else. You would not notice that you had been given his life; you would think that you had been Damon Hill all along. No-one would notice any change, and there seems to be no reason to think that there really has been a change. Swapping selves independently of anything else like this appears to be meaningless. This lends support to the idea that there is no self that is separate from the specific conscious experience produced by a brain.

What are Zuboff's reasons for going in the direction of universalism? Zuboff would probably agree with some of what is presented here: that any boundaries of selfhood beyond those in these two extreme possibilities are arbitrary. But why does he choose universalism over the view that specific experiences are separate selves? His

---

[54] p. 367, italics in original

argument is that if the definition of each self were so specific, most selves would never come into existence. Zuboff (1990) argues that from your own point of view, you would have to side with the theory that makes your existence likely:

> Suppose for a moment that your existence had required a detailed type, such as a particular pattern of experience, memory or genetic coding. Then there would have been an enormous coincidence attached to yours having been a pattern that occurs naturally. Of all the types that might have a priori defined someone's identity, yours would have happened to be one of the incredibly small proportion reflective of the actual order of nature.[55]

Perhaps it could be that those selves who do exist have indeed been very lucky. But this is an unsatisfactory answer, and in his paper, Zuboff goes to great lengths to show why you should always side with the possibility that makes your existence more likely, particularly where the difference in probabilities between the two possibilities is immense, as in this case.

In doing so, Zuboff invokes the Anthropic Principle. In its most basic form, it is the idea that our observations of the universe must be compatible with the existence of observers. Stated like this, it might seem self-evident, but anthropic reasoning is a class of reasoning that makes claims of varying degrees of strength related to an observer's point of view. It involves reasoning from your own existence and your position in the grand scheme of things. Zuboff argues that given the data of your existence, any theory that makes your existence more probable makes that theory proportionally more viable, all other things being equal. Since the theory that every conscious experience is yours makes your existence very likely indeed (it just requires the existence of any conscious experience at all), Zuboff argues in favour of universalism on this basis. This is an example of anthropic reasoning.

However, it could be that more conscious experiences exist naturally than Zuboff gives credit for. This would include the possibility that there are more universes than just this one, which could

---

[55] p. 52

cater for these extra minds. This would make your mind a likely occurrence under either theory, especially since we concluded that identical minds are the same mind and the same self.

The arguments for universalism do not hold any water for a third-person observer, such as the robot Prarnt. Obviously Prarnt was designed merely as an observer of the physical, but we can give it an upgrade that allows it to make basic philosophical observations. It would watch Zuboff drawing the conclusion of universalism based on the fact that he exists. But Prarnt would dismiss these arguments out of hand, even if it went along with the existence of an epiphenomenal consciousness as a premise. The problem is that the arguments are egocentric, and could be made regardless of the truth of universalism. Zuboff would be making the same argument whichever theory is true, and Prarnt would conclude that this is fallacious reasoning. Zuboff, however, is arguing from a different perspective from Prarnt. Anthropic reasoning is not quite so easily written off, and further examples of this form of reasoning will feature in the final chapter of this book.

However, when I wonder why I am not somebody else, there is at least a sense in which it is objectively true that I am not somebody else. I have these thoughts and feelings, and this is what I am. If there is a sense in which I encompass all of consciousness, Zuboff requires that this be the objective truth of the matter, rather than just another way of defining things.

Where should we stand on this: universalism, or the view that each conscious experience is a separate self? If one self has many separate conscious experiences, then there must be something that connects them all together to make them belong to one self – a sort of container. But where does this container come from, and what sort of thing is this container? We have the experiences themselves, and by Ockham's Razor we should not decide that there is something over and above these that somehow links them all together unless there is a very strong reason to. Under universalism, the self would be a further epiphenomenon (since there is no way to detect it) riding on top of the already epiphenomenal mind. This seems to be an epiphenomenon too far. He may deny it, but Zuboff is an epiphenomenalist, although not in the usual sense. If I went down the route of universalism, I would be a double-epiphenomenalist. However, while I am concluding against it, I am sympathetic to universalism, and do sometimes lie awake at night wondering if it is the solution to all our problems. And I will return to it briefly in the final chapter.

I would say that the considerations from this chapter strongly indicate that there is nothing real, that we might call a self, above and beyond specific conscious experiences. Any change in consciousness effectively creates a different self, as it creates a different conscious experience. And as already discussed, any identical minds, whether at the same or at different times, would be the same self. You and your identical copies from the thought experiments would, therefore, have just one self between you while you were identical, but as soon as you diverged, you would have separate selves. And none would be able to claim to be the original self any more than any of the others, as you would all now be different from the original.

We now have our defining feature of the self, although as discussed in chapters 8 and 9, pinning down where a specific conscious experience begins and ends is not exactly trivial, and there is still the possibility of overlapping selves. There are also a couple of further problems relating to personal identity that I will address in the final chapter.

British philosopher Derek Parfit (2002) argues that any questions that still remain once you know all the physical facts are just questions of language.

> Suppose that I know the facts about what will happen to my body, and about any psychological connections that there will be between me now and some person tomorrow. I may ask, 'Will that person be me?' But that is a misleading way to put my question. It suggests that I don't know what's going to happen. When I know these other facts, I should ask, 'Would it be correct to call that person me?' That would remind me that, if there's anything that I don't know, that is merely a fact about our language. [...] It is quite uninteresting whether, with half its components replaced, I still have the same audio system. In the same way, we should regard it as quite uninteresting whether, if half my body were simultaneously replaced, I would still exist.[56]

---

[56] p. 660

Ultimately, Parfit has ended up in a similar place to me. Once you conclude that there is nothing special about personal identity that carries through from one conscious state to the next, you are left with definitions. However, I would certainly not assume from the outset that it is merely a question of language. Consciousness is not the same as the physical, so knowing all the physical facts does not tell you everything about consciousness, including personal identity, so I do not agree with the way that Parfit has come to his conclusion. It is certainly clear, however, that when it comes to the identity of physical objects that have had parts changed over time (such as the Ship of Theseus), there is no philosophical significance, beyond semantic games, to whether you label it as the same object.

This may all seem rather crazy, and far removed from what one might consider to be a 'common-sense' view on personal identity. However, I'm not sure that there is a coherent common-sense view. People often relate their own chances of existence to the chances of the right sperm meeting the right egg in every generation in their ancestry. But even that's not enough. Identical twins are the result of the same sperm/egg combinations, and yet they are different people. So perhaps these people should also be thinking about the fact that for every birth where there were not twins or even more, the right individual was born each time from the many possibilities. But then, does it even make sense to talk about which of the potential twins was born after a zygote does not split? How many potential identities are there? Two, three, an infinite number? And this is only the start of the problems. I'm not going to begin to attempt to piece together a coherent common-sense theory on personal identity, because I do not think that one could exist. But I will leave it as an exercise for the reader to prove me wrong.

Of course, from an everyday language point of view, we do not need to change the way we speak, and we can still talk about our selves lasting the life of our bodies. This is fine, as long as we do not put too much philosophical significance into it. A conscious mind could be seen as like a gravitational field surrounding a large mass. Is it the same field at a later time? It is not literally 'the same one' unless nothing has changed physically, but you might call it the same for convenience. The gravitational field would actually change less than your consciousness 'field', so in that respect has more of a case for being called the same one over time, but I would argue that it is the same general principle. It comes down to semantics, and it seems that there is nothing more tangible than that to your own personal identity over time, now that we have rejected the second layer of epiphenomenon that is universalism.

Personal identity is a topic that might come up in discussions more and more frequently in the future, as technology develops. We might be able to buy brain add-ons, which enhance our mental performance, or have our brains replaced bit-by-bit with silicon chips, or have our minds entirely uploaded onto a computer, or onto many computers. Perhaps we will be teleported by having our bodies destroyed and then recreated in a far-away place out of different matter. How comfortable people are with these ideas is likely to correlate with their views on personal identity.

There is still an unanswered question. In the thought experiment where the scientists claim that they are going to make 99 copies of you 100 years in the future, and you still wake up in the present anyway, do you take it as evidence that the scientists do not finish the experiment? I'm actually going to postpone this yet again, since there is still other ground that needs to be covered. But I will answer it in the final chapter!

Chapter 11

Free Will

Free will is a concept related to consciousness, but it can be a difficult concept to define precisely. However, these are two aspects I consider to be essential to it:

1. If someone has free will, they have the ability to make a conscious decision that is not predictable by anyone, however much information about the situation someone might have. The decision is non-deterministic.
2. The decision and the unpredictability of it must not be due to random chance.

Essentially free will is the ability to make a conscious choice that is both non-random and non-deterministic. This means that if you could replicate a situation exactly, then someone with free will would, in the replicated situation, be able to make a different decision to their exact replica that had gone before: a difference that is caused by their consciousness and that is not influenced by any external factors or because their consciousness is in any way working at random. This is an important point; by saying that free will is not random or deterministic, we are looking for a 'third way'.

There are people who hold that free will is compatible with determinism (known as compatibilists), but this is not the case for the strong definition being used here. This follows automatically from the first defining property mentioned above: that a free decision cannot be predicted. If determinism is true, then free will does not exist. The universe may well not be deterministic anyway, and my arguments do not depend on the specific nature of the universe.

Obviously if epiphenomenalism is correct, then free will cannot exist, as consciousness would have no effect, free or otherwise. However, it is best to start afresh with arguments specific to free will to make for a stronger case.

One argument against the existence of free will mentioned in a *Routledge Encyclopedia of Philosophy Online* article on the subject (Strawson, 1998, 2011) is that since no-one can be the author of themselves, they cannot be responsible for themselves, or for their actions. The argument specifically mentions moral responsibility, but it is the lack of free will that makes the argument work:

> When one acts, one acts in the way one does because of the way one is. So to be truly morally responsible for one's actions, one would have to be truly responsible for the way one is: one would have to be *causa sui*, or the cause of oneself, at least in certain crucial mental respects. But nothing can be *causa sui* – nothing can be the ultimate cause of itself in any respect. So nothing can be truly morally responsible.[57]

In fact, there are many good arguments against free will, and I am not going to hide my position on the subject. So without delay, I will present my own statistical argument against its existence.

Imagine that someone is at a junction, and they have to choose whether to go left or right. The situation is set up many times, with exactly the same starting conditions each time. This means that each individual involved is an exact replica of the others. It is not the same person going into the experiment with the experience and memories of the other occasions.

Suppose for the moment that free will does exist and that the person does not always choose the same direction. Out of the first 1,000 goes, he chooses left 700 times, and right 300 times. What does this mean? If there were a 50% chance of choosing left or right each time, you would expect approximately 500 lefts and 500 rights. But choosing 700 lefts is significantly more than this. Statistically, it is highly unlikely that you will get this many more lefts than rights by chance. It would seem that in this particular case, for some reason

---

[57] Italics in original

there is more chance of the person choosing left than right. You could run a few thousand or a few million more trials to see what the probabilities are more accurately. Whether it is 50% for each direction or skewed towards one more than the other does not matter. What we now have is a reasonable estimate of a probability.

Perhaps you think that the probability model would not describe the situation accurately. Perhaps you could run one million trials and find 999,993 lefts, and then run another one million and find the situation reversed by having only 7 lefts (evening the numbers out over all the trials), because people might just happen to choose differently due to having free will. That *could* happen, but it could also happen if there were a strict 50/50 chance on each occasion. It would just be highly unlikely – in either case. If there are two million independent trials, and you know that in one million of these trials left is chosen, and in the other million right is chosen, then the probability that 999,993 of the lefts will all fall within the first million is virtually zero, and equally so whether it is down to free will or random chance. This is guaranteed by the independence of the trials.

This means that with someone's supposedly free choice, you could make a reasonable estimate of the probability of each decision before the choice was made, based on identical situations previously set up. I chose a situation with just two choices for simplicity, but this would also apply to more complicated situations with any number of choices. We could find our probability distribution by having the situation set up as many times as we needed.

We could form a probability distribution for any supposedly free situation as accurately as we liked, depending on how many trials we chose to observe. We could have a situation where, 99% of the time, a certain choice is made. For the next trial, you might want to say that the person has a free choice, but you would know that there is a 99% chance that one particular option will be chosen, and you could use your statistical knowledge to put money on it.

This supposed free will would be no different from random choices determined by a specific probability function. And therefore it *would be* random choices determined by a specific probability function. But going by the defining properties of free will set out at the start of this chapter, random chance is not free will. Free will requires that choices be made in a way that cannot be represented probabilistically. But there is no room in logical space for this. Therefore, free will cannot exist. There is no conceivable 'third way' outside determinism and randomness.

To make the point clearer, imagine that you do have free will. Now imagine a being that is created to be functionally equivalent to you, but scientists do not know how to create free will, so they instead give it a 'random will' using a module where choices are based on various probability distributions. As I have shown, there should be no problem in principle preventing this creation from being functionally equivalent to you, since random chance can represent any so-called free will that you might have quite adequately. But then, in what sense are you more free than your non-free twin? In no sense. In this example, we have not really done anything except exchange one functional part with another part that differs in only its name.

There is absolutely no room left for the existence of free will. It does not, and cannot, exist. Not in any meaningful, strong sense of the term at least. Not in any way that isn't like defining 'world peace' to be 'a ham sandwich', to borrow David Chalmers's example again. There are, of course, people who use slightly weaker definitions of 'free will' and so conclude that it exists, but these weaker definitions are arguably just describing 'will', rather than 'free will'. The 'free' part has to refer to something extra, otherwise its existence in the phrase cannot be justified. And with a weaker definition, it is no longer a philosophically interesting problem, as free will would just trivially exist. Also, a free will in the strong sense is a minimum requirement for there to be any question of genuine moral responsibility, and for the idea that actions alone deserve punishments or rewards irrespective of considerations such as encouragement, deterrent or any other related reasons.

But as with personal identity, and the term 'self', 'free will' can be used in everyday language quite harmlessly as long as the user doesn't try and take it too far.

Before we finish on the subject, I want to have a brief look at the role that people think free will plays in our lives, but we have to make clear a couple of things first. Our personalities have been determined by our evolutionary history and our environment during our lives. More specifically, they are contained by our brains, in physical form. So, for example, when you do something that is considered by others to be good or bad, it is effectively because you are programmed that way.

Someone might do something that observers think is totally irrational, and the observers can't understand why that person did it. Why would a conscious free-will-owning person act like that? The observers don't understand the action perhaps because they are thinking about it in the wrong way. A brain can be programmed for any behaviour while being just as conscious and having the same perception of having free will.

In some cases of irrational or criminal behaviour, an obvious physical defect in the brain, such as a tumour, is found. This is sometimes used as a defence and a reason to argue that someone isn't responsible for their actions. However, all the causes of our behaviour are physical, and just because in some cases we can find the physical cause, it doesn't mean that there isn't equally a physical cause in all other cases. The more we discover about neuroscience and potential defects in the brain, the more these causes will be found and perhaps the more they will be used as a defence in court. But maybe one day, people will put two and two together and realise that there is always a physical cause, and therefore an equal defence, even in the cases where we haven't discovered it.

It seems that there is a general thought that consciousness and free will inevitably push us all in basically the same direction regarding such things as morality, which is what makes some people's behaviour so difficult to understand. You might think that becoming conscious enables you to see things as they are and make rational and moral decisions. But there is no big overriding controller of behaviour above the mechanistic brain. Our brains control our behaviour, and there is nothing to stop a thinking being from having morals that are completely repugnant to us, as long as its brain is physically wired up in the correct way for this to happen. Evolution and the environment dictate that this does not normally get too far out of control in humans, but it is not stopped by something 'bigger than the brain', which is how people may perceive consciousness or free will.

If beings were created or bred, rather than having evolved naturally, then the creator or breeder could design or breed them to be as irrational as he liked, while still having the same levels of intelligence, consciousness and apparent free will. Our consciousness, our conscience, and our perception of free will are all caused by complex physical brain processes, and do not have any special powers of their own allowing them to overrule the mechanistic brain. There are no shortcuts to complex behaviour.

Part 3
Speculations

Chapter 12

Problems with Consciousness

The whole concept of consciousness and our commitment to epiphenomenalism may seem problematic at the moment but, unfortunately, it gets worse before it gets better. By taking functionalism to its logical conclusions, I will show that it can put into doubt the consciousness/brain link, and even the existence of the outside world.

Causation is considered by many to play an important role in determining consciousness. It is important to emphasise that this is not the same as suggesting that history is important in determining consciousness, as discussed in the Swampman example in chapter 6. With Swampman, it was suggested that events that happened a long time previously might have an effect on current consciousness, despite not being represented in the physical system. But here, we are talking about the current causal properties of a brain state – essentially what future events it can cause to happen – not the dim-and-distant past cause of the current state of affairs. In this sense, Swampman would have the same causal properties as the original Davidson. I will start by considering the case of static objects to illustrate how important causation seems to be in a reasonable theory connecting matter and consciousness.

Static Objects

The thoughts of a conscious mind would normally follow on from each other and change through time (ignoring, for simplicity, any concerns about the continued personal identity of this mind). We can upset this slightly by considering Douglas Hofstadter's book of Einstein's brain again. Obviously any changes made to this book would be through time, but 'Einstein' would not experience time at the same rate as us. We could work through the book at any pace we wanted and have periods of years where we did nothing at all before coming back to it. But as long as we followed instructions correctly, 'Einstein' would not experience any delays at all, but would experience time as if it were flowing normally.

It seems that we can play about with our use of time when considering the flow of a conscious mind, but does the medium of change have to be time at all? This might sound like a strange question, but perhaps a system that would normally change through time could be represented at a single time by a static object. An information-preserving two-dimensional depiction of a three-dimensional object could be made, and then the third spatial dimension could be used to represent time. But would anything be lost here? Would, for example, this system have the same causation as one that changes through time? Is time important for causation? Is causation important for consciousness? According to Einstein's theory of relativity, time is just one of the four dimensions of space-time. And according to at least some interpretations, if we could view the whole of space and time from outside, it would be like looking at a static four-dimensional object. This is known as the 'Block Universe' view. It is only from our perspective that time appears to be flowing. I will continue for now as if time and space are equivalent in this way.

If everything in space-time were represented using just space, including the causes and effects, then the representation would be an isomorphic one and so nothing would be lost. We would simply be representing causation through space rather than time, even if this is a counterintuitive notion. Maybe it seems wrong to talk about cause and effect when there is space but no time. All we have is a static object and nothing is causing anything, but it could be argued that all that this demonstrates is that causation does not really exist even in time, as the whole of space-time can itself be viewed as a static object. Whether this does in fact show that causation exists in neither case or in both cases could come across as a semantic point but, for the time being, I will talk about causation as if it is real in both cases. We do not actually need to invoke Einstein's theory of relativity here. The possibility of being able to isomorphically represent time spatially, at least in certain cases, does not depend on whether time and space are viewed physically as space-time in a correct theory of physics. But I think it helps to illustrate the point. We can easily see that a cylinder can represent a circle existing unchanged over time, regardless of discoveries in physics in the early twentieth century.

By considering just static objects, the situation has been simplified, and it helps us to illustrate just how easy it becomes to represent anything we want. For example, a plain black square could be seen as a black drawing of anything on a black background. The black drawing is there just as much as it would be if the black background were not there, and any properties possessed by the black drawing would be present in both cases. Moving into three dimensions, and using an example from Douglas Hofstadter and Daniel Dennett (1981b, p. 212, although not their intended use for the example), a block of marble could be seen as an exact copy of Michelangelo's *David* that hasn't been unpacked yet. The fact that you wouldn't notice it as being there doesn't change anything. So if a certain complex object were used to represent a human brain changing through time, that object would no less be there if it were surrounded by 'packaging', and all we had was a solid uniform block. It may not contain any information in any useful manner, but it is undeniably there objectively, or at least in the same sense that any static object can be said to objectively contain information. You can find any pattern in any object if you look at it in the right way. It does not matter if the thing being interpreted also happens to be surrounded by black or by marble or indeed whatever else you may choose.

In chapter 6, I discussed the possibility that some interpretation systems might be more arbitrary than others, and that with some, most of the information is arguably in the interpretation system rather than the thing being interpreted, as claimed by Poundstone and Hofstadter. Possibly only the least arbitrary of these systems results in consciousness, which was one way that I suggested to avoid multiple conscious minds arising from a single brain. I rejected the idea at the time, but I am bringing it up here again to make it clear that it could not save us here anyway. With a black square or a marble block, things can still be represented in the least arbitrary or simplest way. It just happens that the thing being interpreted also happens to be surrounded by black or by marble. This is nothing to do with complex or arbitrary interpretation systems.

If we accept that two physically different but functionally equivalent objects can have the same consciousness (e.g. a normal human brain and a silicon-chip brain), we accept that it is some pattern of the object that is important rather than the exact physical make-up. And if we also accept that time does not have any special properties that are not also possessed by space, then we are forced to accept that any pattern can be found in any thing, and so any object could be used as a static representation of a human brain changing through time, with all the correct causation.

This would lead to the conclusion that all objects would have all possible conscious experiences. This would be a most extreme form of panpsychism. Most people would probably be quite happy to accept that any pattern can be found in any thing, but only in a trivial and useless way, until you point out the potential implications of it. Then they might backtrack!

Since all objects would have all consciousness, your own conscious experiences would be part of the consciousness of all objects. And since the occurrence of your consciousness in random objects would by far outnumber its occurrence in brains, it would mean that it is overwhelmingly probable your particular consciousness has been brought about by some random object, rather than by a brain. Well, it would if we had not already drawn the conclusion that identical minds are the same mind (chapter 10), meaning that your mind would equally belong to all objects. But it does show that all conscious experiences can exist while not reflecting in any meaningful manner the physical world and what is happening, even when we consider only those minds that appear to themselves to be in a realistic world. Therefore your senses cannot be trusted to reflect reality.

We believe that brains cause our consciousness because it fits in with what our senses tell us. We also believe in an outside world because our senses convince us that there is one. But if we have good reason to suspect that these senses do not reflect reality, then we are left with no reason to believe our initial assumptions about consciousness being caused by brains, or to believe in a physical outside world at all.

Of course, we are still not fully committed to the idea that time can be fully represented by space. However, perhaps those of us not wanting to make that commitment are in even deeper water when we consider these black squares or marble blocks pointing through time rather than space. For example, a black line existing for a certain amount of time would be isomorphic to a black square, if time were used instead of a second spatial dimension. Likewise, a square marble surface existing through time would represent a solid marble block and anything that the block itself might represent. We could even do away with our reliance on dimension-reducing representations altogether and have a solid block existing for a certain period of time to give ourselves a proper four-dimensional space-time model. Obviously we would have to come up with some sort of exchange rate concerning distance and time, but that's just minor detail. By doing this, we are now using time to represent time again, rather than relying on space as a substitute.

Perhaps this idea would sidestep any dimension-based prejudices, and show that we would find any conscious mind in any static object anyway, now that we are using time in our descriptions. This is an interesting point, but I think that if we were to concede the point that causation has to be through time rather than space, we may also have to accept that this causation would have to use time in a specific way, rather than bluntly pointing an object through it. Just pointing our square or block through time may not automatically involve it in the right sort of time-based causation. At least, it is something to think about.

It seems that the only way to avoid the conclusion that all consciousness can be found in any object would be to argue that time does have special properties not possessed by space, specifically properties to do with causation, so that the Block Universe cannot fully represent the physical state of affairs. There is some controversy as to whether the Block Universe view properly represents space and time, and relativity and quantum mechanics are yet to be unified in this regard. See Slezak (2013) for a recent (at the time of writing) discussion of current theories and controversies in how to view time. Perhaps there is still a way out for causation. However, it does seem to rely on the premise that any static, objective, outside view of completed space-time, perhaps with alternate-future branches where necessary, is either impossible in principle, or at least in some way not equivalent to how things actually are. This is something that you may or may not see as reasonable.

This may also seem slightly unsatisfactory as a get-out as it seems to rely on physics turning out to be a certain way, which could come back to bite us, even if it arguably does make the theory more empirically testable.

Without holding onto the exclusivity of time-based causation, we would appear to have a consciousness free-for-all, causing the Mind–Body Problem to potentially collapse altogether. But even if we do somehow manage to avoid this particular consciousness free-for-all, there is more to come.

Causation, Proximity and Meta-Brains

Let's go back and think of causation in its normal time-based setting. My job here is to bring into doubt the relevance of causation in determining conscious states, even without considering the problem of static objects.

Imagine a brain whose neurons are firing at random, but by chance they just happen to fire as ordinary neurons would. This is different from Zuboff's randomly firing shell discussed in previous chapters, because in this case, all neurons are represented rather than just an outer layer. Obviously the causation would not be the same as in a normal brain, so according to a theory of consciousness based on causation, we would not accept that this brain has the same consciousness as a normal brain.

If proximity of neurons (that they are all in the same location) is not relevant to consciousness, then it does not matter where the neurons are. If causation is not important either, then as long as the neurons were firing at the right times, it would not matter whether the firings had any bearing on each other. We could pick any set of neurons from any set of brains in the world and call it a meta-brain. There will always be countless neurons firing at the same time (or near enough to make no difference) as each neuron in your brain. Having said that, when the firing happens should not be important; the relevant firing pattern would still exist, albeit in a more complex way, if the timings were changed. For each experience caused by a specific neural firing pattern within one brain, there would be countless identical representations caused by meta-brains. If proximity and causation are not important for consciousness, then the meta-brains would also be conscious.

As with the case of static objects, in which any pattern can be found, the overwhelming majority of meta-brains would produce experiences that do not meaningfully reflect the real world and what is happening, even if you include only the ones that appear to themselves to be in an ordered universe. As before, your senses could not be trusted to reflect reality, and again we would be left with reduced reason to even believe in the outside world.

We have already seen the implications of accepting the existence of causation in static objects, so nothing here should shock you. So let's look at whether proximity and causation are relevant to consciousness, starting with proximity.

In 'The Story of a Brain' by Arnold Zuboff (1981), there is a project called the 'Great Experience Feed' in which the neurons of a man's brain are separated and spread out over space. Each neuron is still connected up to the others using transmitters and receivers, and each neuron is in a nutrient bath, with a man responsible for firing it. The neurons are fired in the sequence in which they would fire in a normal brain for certain experiences to occur.

In this situation, every neuron is fired at the right time and they are all causally connected in the right manner.[58] The brain is functioning in the same way as a normal brain. The only thing that has

---

[58] In the story as it is told, it would seem that the neurons are actually being fired at set times, rather than due to any causal link-up between them. If this is what Zuboff meant, we can easily imagine a slightly modified scenario where they are causally connected as in a normal brain.

changed is the neurons' proximity. There is no reason that I can see to suggest that the distance between the neurons should in any way affect the consciousness of the brain, if everything else is kept constant. If the physical distance does matter, where is the line drawn? How close would neurons have to be to each other for the brain to be conscious? Distance simply does not seem relevant as long as the neurons are still able to fire properly. The neural pattern is still the same, so using our own conclusions on functionalism and the interpretations of brain states, we would have to conclude that consciousness is unaffected by the proximity of neurons.

Of the two candidates, proximity was never the more likely one to stop meta-brains from being conscious, but I wanted to be explicit about what variables I am going to play about with.

The Argument from Horse Racing

Imagine that instead of having random neurons, there are modules that affect the firing of each neuron in a way that depends on the results of certain horse races. These are super-fast horse races, of course, and millions can take place each second. Each neuron is tied up to a particular set of these horse races. It could be, for example, that the winner of each horse race determines what happens to the transmission signal (what enters the synaptic gap – the gap between neurons) of one particular neuron for one second. Each horse has attached to it certain information about what should happen to the neuron should it win the race. If the right horse wins, then the signal from that neuron will be unaffected for that second. In each race, a horse that will not upset the neuron's signal is known as an identity horse. Identity horses aren't planted in the races – there just happen to be enough horses with all sorts of potential effects in each race that each race contains at least one identity horse anyway. It could be fixed so that all of the races are won by identity horses. In this case, causation would not be affected, so consciousness should not be either. Now imagine the case where the results are not fixed, but all the races happen to be won by identity horses anyway.

Scenario 1: The neurons' connections are rerouted and the transmission signals (or lack of) from each neuron over the course of one second are wiped out and replaced with a new set of signals that are entirely dependent on the result of a horse race. The original transmission signals are irrelevant to the end result. In the case of an identity horse winning, the new output signals that are created are identical to the original transmission signals.

Scenario 2: Instead of the signals being rerouted to begin with, they are only modified if an identity horse does not win. The horse-race system is effectively floating above the brain, and not in physical contact, and only intervenes when a race is not won by an identity horse.

In scenario 1, the neurons are no longer causally connected, and on the assumption that causation is important for consciousness, the consciousness would be drastically altered or even eliminated. In scenario 2, if identity horses win every race, nothing is done to the brain at all. Yet it seems that it is a functionally and causally equivalent system to the one described in scenario 1, which just happens to have a different implementation. If consciousness is lost in scenario 1, it seems absurd to suggest that we might be committing ourselves to saying that the intact brain in scenario 2 also loses its consciousness due to a causal possibility floating above it. On the flipside, if scenario 2 leaves consciousness intact, does it follow that the same must apply in the functionally and causally equivalent scenario 1, meaning that causation cannot be relevant to consciousness?

Fortunately it is not that simple. While it may be that scenario 1 and scenario 2 describe functionally and causally equivalent systems, scenario 2 also has a subsystem that is a normal human brain. Scenario 1 does not have this subsystem. It may be that each of the two systems as a whole do not have normal human consciousness, but that the normal-brain subsystem in scenario 2 is still as conscious as ever.

Causation has survived this attack. But let's look in more detail at the difference between replacing a signal with an identical one by chance, and letting it pass through unchanged. The line between treating this as a normal causal brain and treating it as a random brain or a meta-brain is finer than you might think, and possibly non-existent.

Firstly, it should not make any difference if the new signal is created from the same molecules as the one that's just been destroyed, or from different molecules, as identical matter should be viewed as isomorphic, and causation isn't dependent on specific matter. Indeed, we could imagine a normal causal case where the signal molecules are replaced with identical ones along the way. The specific molecules involved are not important here, meaning that we cannot causally distinguish between the same signal and a merely identical one on these grounds.

In scenario 1, where the signal is replaced, we could use the same matter for the replacement signal, purely by chance, as the new signal is created indiscriminately using matter that happens to be in the vicinity. Does it make any difference if we actually separate the molecules that make up the signal and put them back together again, or could we just remove the whole signal intact and put it back again as we found it, even if this all happened by chance? If it does make a difference, how far apart do we have to pull the molecules before it makes a difference, and how far away from the transmitting neuron do we have to move them before putting them back again? There seems to be no answer that isn't entirely arbitrary, and so leaving the system unchanged can be viewed as the same as removing the signal, tearing it up and replacing it with a new one that happens to be the same. It now appears that there is no way to reasonably distinguish between a causal and a random system, which puts causation into further jeopardy.

It could be argued that I was too hasty in condemning the brain in scenario 1 as not conscious. It could be that it does have normal consciousness, because each neuron is in the same causal state as it would be in a normal brain. At the level of the individual neurons, the brain is the same as normal; it is only between the neurons that things have changed. But this would also be the case if we had the right number of completely unconnected neurons across many different brains that happened to be in the right causal states, such as in a meta-brain. To be clear, the neurons in a meta-brain are just as causally connected to each other as the neurons in the brain in scenario 1 are to each other. So this does not offer causation a reasonable way out. What happens between the neurons is important.

Another Route for Causation?

Perhaps what we need is a causal connection between neurons that runs deeper than anything we have previously considered here. But there are very limited options for this. Some might suggest quantum entanglement, but I'm not sure that this would solve the problem, and it would add many more of its own. Roger Penrose and Stuart Hameroff argue for a quantum theory of consciousness (e.g. Penrose, 1994; Hameroff & Penrose, 1996), involving the micro-tubules inside neurons, but they have approached it from a different direction. I discussed some of Penrose's reasoning in chapter 2.

Keeping causation as an important factor in consciousness production seems to be very problematic, and when one considers what is involved, one might be tempted to invoke Ockham's Razor and slice the whole thing apart, especially considering that the most obvious solution to each problem seems to involve hijacking quantum physics for philosophical means, something which has a long and ugly history.

But if we gave up on it, it seems that we would have to concede that meta-brains are as conscious as we are, which could lead us to doubt the existence of the outside world. Causation and the consciousness/physical link are now firmly on the back foot. Let's also not forget that I have concluded that there could be no physical evidence for the existence of consciousness, so we are looking for a physical implementation for something that is essentially a purely philosophical idea. We should not necessarily expect there to be a reasonable solution. It is difficult to know where to go from here, so I think it is time to start questioning some of our initial assumptions regarding consciousness and physics.

Chapter 13

Further Speculation and Conclusions

In this final chapter I will draw together the conclusions from the earlier chapters and provide a few further thoughts to reach some bigger conclusions about consciousness. I have discussed many aspects of consciousness and gone in all sorts of directions, and caused all sorts of problems for myself, so now it is time to try and tie together what we have discovered along the way. The assumptions of physics and the consciousness/physical link are open to discussion in this chapter.

I concluded in chapter 5 that there can never be any third-person scientific evidence for the existence of consciousness. I also concluded in the same chapter that if there is a consciousness/physical link, then it must be an epiphenomenal link. Consciousness has no effect in the physical world, even if it results from the physical itself. Then in chapter 12, the viability of the whole Mind–Body Problem was questioned. The conclusion of functionalism from chapter 4 commits us to a theory of consciousness based on a pattern of the brain (interpretationalism), and since any pattern can be found in any thing from the Block Universe perspective (as argued in chapter 12), we may not be able to trust our own conscious senses, and it is these senses that lead us to believe that there is a consciousness/physical link in the first place. Indeed, it is these senses that lead us to believe that there is a physical world beyond our own minds. One possible escape route that I mentioned is to argue that the Block Universe view of space-time has fundamental limitations and that time-based causation could therefore still hold a special reserve, limiting what can be considered functionally or interpretationally equivalent. However, even more pressure was put on a consciousness based on causation by the Argument from Horse Racing.

The problems that we have encountered while trying to find a connection between consciousness and physical matter could lead one to give up on consciousness altogether and go in the direction of zombic materialism. I concluded in chapter 5 that this is the best solution if you are being truly objective, looking at all the evidence from the third-person perspective. You eliminate a lot of problems if you just cut consciousness out altogether, and perhaps we shouldn't expect there to be a reasonable resolution to this unscientific idea. However, this is not a very satisfactory route to take in a book on consciousness. Zombic materialism, moreover, is based on the assumption that matter and physics exist first and foremost, and is the most logical conclusion only under this initial assumption, but it could be argued that this is doing things back to front. After all, it is our senses that lead us to believe in the physical outside world, and our experience of it is only indirect, so the physical world is certainly not the most fundamental thing from our perspective. No direct proof of its existence exists, even if there is a lot of consistent evidence. Perhaps it would be more appropriate to start with the assumption that consciousness exists and, from there, make a conclusion about the physical outside world. The question of the link between consciousness and physics is being reopened.

I concluded in chapter 10 that even if minds do arise from the physical, each mind is not fixed to one physical situation; identical brains would produce the same mind. This applies regardless of time or location. Identical minds, in different places and at different times, are the same mind. They exist as non-physical entities, independent of any specific physical form, or indeed of any specific physical universe, if there are other universes. But since the connection with the physical is now being questioned, we could even envisage the existence of minds as independent of the physical in any way. If minds are dependent on the physical, it is only the pattern that they are dependent on. Perhaps we can take this further than simply the patterns from concretely existing physical objects, as I will demonstrate.

Conceptual Physics – Do Things Actually Have to Happen?

Imagine the following hypothetical event. You cross a road without looking and just avoid being run over by a car. It was a lucky escape but you dwell on what would have happened had you crossed at a very slightly different time. There are certain events that would have taken place if there had been marginally different starting conditions. It would appear, however, that as these events never took place, they are not experienced. But there are still facts about what would have happened, whether anyone can know them or not. The existence of a physical universe is not required for it to be true that if one did exist with certain laws and starting conditions, then certain specific things would follow. Importantly, these facts are as detailed and complex as the real world in which we live. Perhaps these facts alone could be seen as a sort of representation in themselves. This raises an interesting question. Do we require the existence of a real physical universe where the relevant physical pieces are physically moved around for these experiences to be borne out, or can the experience happen regardless of the existence of a physical universe containing the event?

According to a functional theory of consciousness, if the representation were made by a brain in a vat, or by a computer simulation, then this would be enough for the experience to happen, but in these cases there is still a physical representation. Here, we are taking it much further and considering whether a non-physical hypothetical state is enough of a representation in itself to generate the experiences.

With interpretationalism (which follows from functionalism), the mind is the realisation of a possible interpretation of a physical state. There is no-one there to do the interpreting, and it is not clear how or why it is realised in conscious form. We have already moved into the realm of fairly abstract concepts, so I don't think that it is that much more of a leap for the brain state itself to be hypothetical. A non-physical hypothetical idea is just as interpretable as a real physical event. And if a hypothetical or conceptual scenario is enough to generate our conscious experiences (our data), then arguably real, concretely-existing, physical universes are redundant in our explanations, and so could be illusory, even if this is counter-intuitive.

All possible physical universes, with all possible laws of physics, exist as hypotheticals or concepts anyway (in the same way as the various possibilities that never happened in the road-crossing incident), so if this is the only way in which they exist, then this puts all possible universes on an equal footing. If you imagine a wild and crazy universe, it exists as a concept, and so it would therefore exist as much as any other, going by this view.

Consciousness is already non-physical, and cannot exist as a 'lesser form' (it is either experienced or it is not), so it makes no difference to its status if consciousness results from a pattern of concrete physics or a pattern of conceptual physics. This 'demotion' of the physical would not result in an equivalent demotion of consciousness.

All possible physical universes and all possible minds would exist in purely conceptual terms, but this would be all the existence that there is; there would be nothing 'more' than conceptual existence. Since all existence would be fundamental, things would be the only way they could ever be. Nothing arbitrary would ever have happened to create the state of affairs, which would suit Ockham's Razor. The way things are may seem arbitrary and specific to you, but that is because you are seeing, and indeed being, only one part of reality, rather than seeing or being the overall big picture of everything. Also, the idea that it is illogical to believe in consciousness, on the basis that there is no scientific evidence, would no longer apply if this reasoning went through. If we are considering that everything possible might exist, this includes consciousness just as much as it does physical existence. Indeed, we could even consider the possibility of universes where idealism is true and where there is no true physics but just the illusion of it, although arguably this may not be that different from the conceptual physics that we are already considering.

This does have similarities with philosopher David Lewis's Modal Realism (e.g. 1986), but his theory, as I understand it, is that all possible universes exist concretely, whereas I am suggesting that their conceptual existence alone is enough to bring about the entirety of our experience. It is perhaps more similar to physicist Max Tegmark's Mathematical Universe Hypothesis (e.g. 2008),[59] which states that our universe is simply a mathematical structure and that all possible mathematical structures exist in the same way as our universe. In his paper, Tegmark also discusses solutions to various problems with the idea, such as what counts as 'possible' and other more mathematical problems. I am not going to address all of these particular problems here, however.

Perhaps this idea comes across as a bit of a cheat, by trying to create something from nothing. However, I have already concluded that consciousness is a non-physical abstraction anyway, so putting physics onto this level is not necessarily such a big step beyond this. I also see no particular reason why physical existence should trump all other types, and get to be the 'concrete' one, although I make no bones about the fact that this is very speculative.

Statistical Likelihood and Anthropic Reasoning

We are not out of the woods yet. If we are putting conscious minds on an equal conceptual footing with physical universes, then it seems that they can exist independently, rather than having to result from a pattern of conceptual physics. Otherwise, even though it is now conceptual, physics would still seem to trump other types of existence. To achieve equality, and also to avoid the problems from chapter 12, it now seems that we might have to sever the ties between our minds and the world that they apparently inhabit. This, however, creates further problems relating to personal identity. If all minds exist equally, surely most possible minds would be disordered and incoherent, so why is it that your mind is one of the ordered ones that considers itself to be in an ordered universe? A lot of disordered minds could probably be dismissed as conscious noise (as discussed in chapter 6), but we would still be left with a vast number of ordered conscious minds

---

[59] Tegmark (2014) has formulated his ideas into a book, but it was released too late to influence this book.

that perceive themselves to be in a bizarre and disordered universe, or do not perceive themselves to be in a universe at all. For example, there would be individuals who regularly see their friends turn into mushrooms for no apparent reason! But this has never happened to me, or probably you.

One rather blunt way of avoiding this problem of personal identity would be to say that it is equivalent to asking why a sheep is not a cow. Each concept can only be itself and so each conscious mind can only ever be itself. Wondering why it is not something different just doesn't make sense.

However, it is not satisfactory to dismiss the seemingly freak chance that you happen to perceive yourself to be in an ordered universe in such a manner. Think of all the precise laws of physics that you seem to be experiencing, and how ordered the world is. Is this really simply because you are this mind as opposed to that, rather than because there actually are these laws of physics? It would be a terrible intellectual crime to write off all of science in this manner, because that is what we would be doing. We have to be very careful when mixing philosophy with science; philosophical conclusions should not draw us away from the real world, because it makes too much sense! The question 'Why am I me?' is a big philosophical problem and not easily dismissed. This problem could be seen as an argument in favour of Zuboff's universalism that we left behind in chapter 10, since universalism avoids such a blunt answer to the question of why you are your specific mind. However, I consider the arguments against universalism to be fairly strong, and in any case, there is more to say on this subject before we would have to concede anything.

This is where we need to start reasoning anthropically. We need a solution that makes it probable (or at least reasonably likely) for a mind to appear to be in an ordered world. But if all minds simply exist fundamentally, then such an answer appears impossible. On the other hand, reducing minds to being merely secondary concepts, riding on conceptual physics, would seemingly be a retrograde step at this point.

However, there may be a way out of our quandary that avoids severing the ties between consciousness and physics. It could be that conscious minds still are fundamental concepts themselves, but that they also result from the interpretation of physical concepts.

Each mind would exist just once as a fundamental concept and many times as the result of a pattern or patterns in a conceptual physical universe: one for each brain or other object that contains it. The instances of each stand-alone mind would pale into insignificance against the instances of identical minds created by the goings-on in conceptual physical universes, so we would no longer need to worry about the greater number of bizarre minds relative to ordered minds when looking purely at fundamental existence.

This could still seem unsatisfactory because even though I have tried to put both physics and consciousness at an equal level in the conceptual food chain, physics still seems to get its nose in front of consciousness by bringing about most of its existence. We would also reinherit all the problems from chapter 12 relating to causation if consciousness results from physics, even if it is conceptual physics. This was our trigger to look at conceptual physics in the first place (well, I may have presented it as the trigger, but it was always in the plan and was going to happen one way or another). Perhaps worse is that I concluded in chapter 10 that identical minds are the same mind, so it seems to make no sense to talk about different instances of each mind. We will have to address each of these problems in turn, starting with the consciousness/physical 'pecking order'.

It could be that both conceptual physics and consciousness result from the same underlying conceptual or mathematical cause of the universe that they inhabit, rather than physics causing consciousness (or vice versa). This keeps them linked and equal and it would make them both in a sense epiphenomenal. However, it would not be such a major concern if physics did keep its nose in front in the manner discussed. This is more of an aesthetic consideration than anything else.

Additionally, with this solution, as consciousness would not result from the physical manifestation of a concept or mathematical abstraction, but from the underlying concept or abstraction itself, we could also find a possible way round some of the problems encountered in chapter 12 involving physical causation. In a theory where consciousness results from physics, the blind and meaningless physical interactions have to be translated into consciousness, and this is what gave us the problem that any pattern can be found in any thing. What I am suggesting now is that fundamentally meaningful concepts, which possibly do not require extra interpretation, are responsible for our consciousness and our perception of the world around us.

To demonstrate that this would give the statistical results that we need regarding the likelihood of being a mind such as ours, and avoid a consciousness free-for-all, would require a lot more work, however (to be discussed shortly). And we would still arguably be left with exactly the same main problem as before. Although we are no longer concerned with how physical brains cause consciousness, we are still concerned with how conceptual brains are associated with consciousness, even if they are both caused by an underlying abstraction. And we would again be looking at which brains are associated with conscious minds and what the relevant properties of those brains are. What relevant difference is there between ordinary human brains and meta-brains or random brains, if not their causal properties? I do, however, think that this is a worthwhile starting point, even if it may ultimately gain us no ground.

Now for the identity of minds. We concluded in chapter 10 that identical minds are the same mind, regardless of where they come from. So it would seem that the creation of minds from abstract concepts would not add anything new to help us after all, since they all already exist fundamentally and they can only exist once. But there may still be a way round this. Identical fundamental physical particles cannot be said to have their own unique identity. They are effectively the same particle rather than merely identical, and yet we can clearly see that there are many instances of the same one particle in our physical universe. This is known as fungibility. Physicist David Deutsch (e.g. 2012, p. 265) borrows this term from legal terminology for use in physics. It is often used relating to money, in that it makes no sense to talk about which £10 you have withdrawn from your bank, since it is all the same, but there are clearly many instances of £10 (hopefully).

By the same token, perhaps there are many fungible instances of each mind. This is to say that while separate instances of identical brains still do not create minds with any difference in identity, each extra brain creates another fungible instance of the same mind. This could be our mechanism to enable the ordered minds that consider themselves to be in an ordered universe to outnumber the wild and crazy minds and the ordered minds in crazy situations, even though they are less densely populated when considered as individual concepts.

Perhaps a good analogy for why ordered minds might be more abundant is that if you attempt to solve a problem in mathematics, you are far more likely to come across certain numbers, such as 0, 1, e or pi, than most other numbers picked at random. It would be possible to define a system of creating mathematical problems requiring numerical solutions, where the complexity of the problem is defined in terms of setting up the problem: for example, where a problem's complexity is determined by how many characters it takes to set it out clearly in a well-defined system. This form of complexity is known as Kolmogorov complexity. It may then be that for problems up to any finite degree of complexity (where there would be a finite number of problems),[60] certain numerical solutions would by far outnumber other ones.

Similarly, complexity of universes could be defined in terms of such things as complexity of physical laws, number of laws, and

---

[60] I have chosen a finite degree of complexity because it makes it simpler to talk about how likely certain solutions are. If there are an infinite number of mathematical problems, solutions must occur an infinite number of times each, so talking about the likelihood of certain solutions coming up becomes a lot trickier because we are dividing infinity by infinity. That's not to say that it is entirely meaningless, however. If we know the first n digits of pi and none after that, we'd say that from our point of view the $(n+1)$th digit of pi has a 1 in 10 chance of being a 0, and a 9 in 10 chance of being in the range 1–9. Of course, there are only 10 possibilities here so no infinity, but it's not quite that simple. Another way of looking at it is that there are an infinite number of possible combinations of digits from the $(n+1)$th onwards – an infinite number that start with 0, and an infinite number that start with any number from 1–9. But most people would be quite happy to say that it is more likely that a combination that starts with 1–9 is the one that actually occurs. Those that aren't will, I imagine, be willing to take up a series of bets with me about currently unknown digits of pi, with odds set accordingly.

amount of energy and matter (or whatever else may exist in a universe), and it could be that in universes up to any finite level of complexity, certain minds, or certain types of mind, occur far more frequently than others.[61] It may one day be possible to run limited simulations of universes, and put this to the test to see if minds like ours – intelligent, ordered minds that appear to themselves to be in an ordered universe – are commonly occurring. This would be our prediction. There is the question of the frequency of randomly formed Boltzmann brains and whether that might spoil things, but that is a problem that exists anyway even just considering our own universe in a normal physical way. Our prediction would be that Boltzmann brains are rare enough not to cause minds like ours to be less common than is reasonable. Obviously how common they need to be to satisfy us is open to debate, but the same goes for standard statistical hypothesis testing.

Max Tegmark (2008) argues that determining whether our universe is typical for one containing observers like us would be a scientific test for his Mathematical Universe Hypothesis, and the same would apply for the theory I am presenting. We have two separate tests here: firstly Tegmark's test that our universe is typical for one containing intelligent observers, and secondly the test that our own minds are typical of intelligent beings and that they outnumber minds from Boltzmann brains (or at least aren't outnumbered by them by too much).

A third possible test would be the likelihood of a mind being a human-level intelligent mind. We need this to be fairly high for us not to be in too improbable a position ourselves as intelligent minds.

---

[61] There is a problem of whether complexity is, to an extent, a function of the language of description. You can contrive a language in which any universe you want is the simplest to describe. I do risk being hoist by my own petard based on what I said about arbitrary interpretation systems being objectively as correct as any other, but I do think that objective complexity is a different enough topic for there to be some leeway here. If a universe has exactly the same set-up as another except with extra details on top, it could be argued that it is strictly more complex, regardless of a language in which it can be described in a simpler manner. One universe could contain one object, and another universe could contain that object and also another identical object next to it, for example.

As discussed, we would have to compete with the existence of conscious noise, but on top of this there is also the consciousness of other life-forms, such as non-human animals, which would presumably be far greater in number than intelligent conscious minds, such as ours. This could mean that the test has already failed before we even leave Earth!

However, these 'lesser' conscious minds might not cause us so much of a problem, because although there may be more of them by number, the intelligence and richness of human minds presumably mean that we have more in the way of conscious experience than other animals, and so take up a larger area in 'consciousness-space'. It could be that it is likely, or even probable, that if one picked a random point in 'consciousness-space-time' (consciousness-space across all time), one would stumble across an intelligent mind seeing itself in a consistent universe (such as a human mind). Our prediction would be that this likelihood would hold when universes up to any arbitrarily high level of complexity are considered.

I am not arguing that you were created by the picking of a random point in consciousness-space-time. But by picking random points, we can see if we are in an improbably privileged or impoverished position. This type of comparison isn't limited to just humans, and can be used to compare across species. You would not expect to be improbably tall for a human – say, the only person in the world who was over three metres tall – and in the same sense you would not expect to be improbably intelligent for a being in general (i.e. not just for a human). I think it is reasonable to argue this way – otherwise what reason have we got for thinking that we are in any way typical observers? If we have no reason to think that we are typical observers, we could be any sort of bizarre observer, and so we have no reason to trust any of science or the outside world. If not through anthropic reasoning, why do you think that you are not the result of a Boltzmann brain, and so why do you think order in your life will continue beyond this moment? Similarly, Swedish philosopher Nick Bostrom (2002) argues that:

> One should reason as if one were a random sample from the set of all observers in one's reference class.

He later specifies it further:

> One should reason as if one's present observer-moment were a random sample from the set of all observer-moments in its reference class.[62]

By adding 'moment', this tallies with what I have said about consciousness-space-time as opposed to just consciousness-space, although his is more 'conscious-entity'-time, since he is considering each conscious entity as one unit rather than looking at it as an area of consciousness-space. He also argues that we should reason *as if* we are random observers even if we weren't actually picked at random in any way. Bostrom discusses at length what beings should count as being in the same reference class as you – the class that you are considered as a random sample from. Under universalism, since all minds are your mind, it could be seen as making more sense that your current thoughts are a random sample from this. So in some ways, universalism could be seen as handling the problem a bit better than the theory that I am using. But as I mentioned earlier in this chapter, based on everything I've argued and concluded, I'm not about to revert now.

I think it makes sense to consider all minds to be in our reference class for this test, and look at the size of minds rather than just the number of them, in the way I just have. One cannot be a rock if a rock has no consciousness, so one is 'more likely' to be an ant than a rock, however many rocks there are. Similarly, one is more likely to be a specific human than a specific ant, because the amount of consciousness that an ant has is presumably negligible compared to that of a human. This is actually the same reason that we can dismiss what I've called conscious noise, as I have done a few times throughout this book. I suggested at the end of chapter 6 that we might be able to dismiss bizarre minds that result from our brain because they are statistically outnumbered by ordered minds, but it might be more reasonable to say that the area they take up in consciousness-space is negligible compared to that of ordered minds. To continue

---

[62] p. 162

the point, one could even make comparisons between different humans, but I'll leave that as an exercise for the reader.

Something we could do now is devise a relevant measure of psychological consciousness, perhaps based on cognitive power, and apply the consciousness-space-time test to life on Earth since it started, based on our knowledge of our own and other species. To be explicit, we would calculate the proportion of consciousness-space-time that is taken up by humans. This could be a way of telling how statistically improbable our position is as intelligent beings, given that we are on Earth. If results from this test indicate that we have been incredibly lucky even on Earth, then it might not be a brilliant test to take forward into other realms. But if, as I would hope, the results do not show us to be so lucky, then perhaps this test can be applied across the rest of the universe and even to simulations of other universes (if we can achieve such advanced simulations). In effect, we are testing the test before applying it.

Here we can revisit Giulio Tononi's information integration theory of consciousness, which we first encountered in chapter 9. According to his theory, amount of consciousness, Φ, is measured by the amount of information that a system can integrate. This could perhaps be an interesting starting point for our measure of consciousness in our test. In Tononi's book *Phi: A Voyage from the Brain to the Soul* (2012) – a fictional tale of Galileo on a journey of discovery – Galileo swaps his telescope for a qualiascope, and from this perspective (essentially the perspective of consciousness-space), a moth or a firefly is much larger and brighter than a whole star (see pp. 212–225).

If the consciousness-space-time test passes its own initial test and is to be taken as valid, then it can be used for more than making predictions about other universes under the assumption that all possible universes exist conceptually. For example, we can use it to make predictions about the likelihood of human-level intelligent life having evolved on other planets in our own universe, on the assumption that animal-type life has evolved. Our prediction would be that if there is animal life on other planets, then intelligent life is common enough on such planets that, when the consciousness-space-time test is applied to the whole universe, it will not put us as intelligent beings in an improbably privileged position. To be clear, if we picked a random point in consciousness-space-time, we would want the probability of finding an intelligent and ordered mind to be reasonably high.

We could also use this test to make predictions about the existence of life-forms with intelligence that far exceeds our own, including perhaps advanced computers, and even deities, if that's where your thinking takes you. We would expect them not to be so common or so advanced that they have too much of a monopoly on consciousness-space-time. We would expect not to be improbably impoverished just as much as we would expect not to be improbably privileged. If we are using consciousness-space-time across all possible space and time, then this includes our own future, so it would also limit the likely number and/or power of super-intelligent computers on Earth in the future, and the human species's cognitive advancement. This would be quite a significant conclusion. It might seem strange to be making predictions about the future in this manner, but I think it is best to think of the future as part of the complete conceptual realm or of complete consciousness-space-time, rather than simply something that hasn't happened yet.

There are other predictions that could be made. If we are expecting to be in a typical position for intelligent life, then our position relative to the age of the universe is also relevant, for example. We would not expect the vast majority of consciousness to be either ahead of or behind us in time, which could possibly help us to predict how far into the future life in the universe will be viable. This would also apply to our existence just on Earth. As with all things, we'd have to decide what counted as a reasonable proportion, but without even having any knowledge of cosmology, it would be a surprising result if it turned out that 99% of the consciousness of the universe, or on Earth, was still to come or had already happened. You can make certain predictions about the future of life in the universe if you have a reasonable knowledge of its past. As you can see, we can use anthropic reasoning in ways that transcend time and space, and I think it is a very powerful and exciting tool.

I originally approached this line of reasoning from scratch. But it turns out that the idea that the future of human life on Earth is limited, based on this form of anthropic probabilistic reasoning, has already been considered, and is known as the 'Doomsday Argument', and there are many arguments for and against it. This and many other anthropic arguments are discussed at length in the book *Anthropic Bias* by Nick Bostrom (2002). It is an interesting, if difficult, read.

Hopefully these considerations provide a potential answer to some of the problems that we have encountered. The question of 'Why am I me?' – rather than a considerably less or more intelligent mind, an incoherent, disjointed mind, or a mind that finds itself living in an incoherent, disjointed world – is addressed in statistical terms, without resorting to Zuboff's universalism. The related problem that identical minds are the same mind, which threatened to undo the statistical work, is dealt with by fungibility. The threat of zombic materialism is dealt with by giving physics and consciousness equal standing in terms of fundamental existence.

The problems of chapter 12 involving causation, random brains, meta-brains and that any pattern can be found in any thing have still not been fully solved, but I have suggested a possible solution, or at least directions to a possible solution, where consciousness and physics both depend on an underlying mathematical abstraction or conceptual realm and are not directly connected to each other.

A Note on Probability

When we consider that minds that are identical to yours are actually the same mind, it would be wrong to say that you have a certain probability of being in a particular type of universe, or being in a computer simulation, or being a brain in a vat etc. It is wrong because it implies that there is an absolute truth of the matter, and that we just don't know the answer yet. The instances of your mind are fungible, so a better way to describe the situation would be to say that a certain proportion of the instances of your mind are in each scenario, even if it is more wordy.

In chapter 10 on personal identity, I asked whether it was possible to effectively see into the future if you woke up in the present, rather than as one of 99 identical copies that were supposed to be made by scientists 100 years in the future. Waking up as you now could lead you to believe that either you have been very lucky or the scientists will not go on to produce the copies in the future. So what is the answer?

Personal identity transcends both time and space, so for the brief moment that the copies are identical to you, you are all the same individual, even if for them that brief moment is 100 years after when the brief moment is for you. The probability of each future outcome for you would be the same as the proportion of the instances of your mind that would lead to that outcome (assuming a continuous self, for simplicity).[63] If the copies are made, then the proportion of the instances where you will find yourself still in the present is very small. So if you do wake up in the present as the original you, then you can take it as evidence against the hypothesis that scientists will complete their experiment and create the copies of you. Bayesian probability will tell you that if there is any chance that the scientists might fail to complete their experiment, then this probability increases if a random sample of one self finds itself in the present. Likewise, waking up in the present when the super-being supposedly made 99 copies of you 1,000 years in the past can be taken as evidence against the hypothesis that it really happened.

However, in this particular case, the evidence is specific to you, and no-one else that you speak to afterwards can share this reasoning, because for them there was always only one possible outcome, namely finding you in the present. Arnold Zuboff (2000) has written a very interesting paper on how probability can vary for different observers with the same information.

Non-Zombic Materialism Revisited

We left behind non-zombic materialism in chapter 5, but I do not think that everyone would be convinced by my arguments. I think it

---

[63] We do not need to make this assumption. Instead of probability, we can talk about the number of selves in each situation as a proportion of those who wake up with memories of having taken part in the experiment. If the scientists complete the experiment, then the proportion waking up in the present is 1%, which is equivalent to the 1% probability in the continuous-self model.

is worth having one final look at it, now that we have further explored the nature of consciousness.

For every logically possible thought experiment that we have encountered, non-zombic materialism would have to have a suitable answer. These are not problems I have caused myself by following epiphenomenalism, but problems for consciousness per se. Only zombic materialism is exempt. Materialism would have to address the possibility of consciousness being found in random brains, meta-brains and static objects. Functionalist materialism (the most popular type) is still reliant on patterns, so would also have to address the problem of any pattern being found in any thing, and therefore of whether we are able to trust our senses. The conclusion (based on functionalist reasoning) that identical minds are the same mind would need to be addressed in physical terms, or refuted. The deeper we go into the problem of consciousness, the more limited and inflexible materialism appears to be.

In a materialist theory, physics would exhaust all of the facts about consciousness. Once we understood everything physical, which objects of those described are conscious and which are not should simply fall into place. But after what we've considered throughout this book, I think this is placing a very heavy burden on physics, and I would not want to be the one claiming that physics will make any announcements on such matters.

I have already drawn what I consider to be strong conclusions on the subject of non-zombic materialism, and have long since left it behind in my own thinking, so I will not provide further arguments, but will leave you with these thoughts.

Final Conclusions

We have come a long way to reach where we are, from finding in favour of functionalism, epiphenomenalism and interpretational-ism, to speculating that all physical existence is nothing more than conceptual existence. This could be seen as a sort of platonism. It could also be seen as idealism or even a neutral monism, although it would depend on your vantage point, and your precise definitions. It is certainly a move away from the type of epiphenomenalist dualism that I started out with, since consciousness is no longer dependent on a concrete physics. However, consciousness would still have no causal powers of its own, so it would still be epiphenomenal.

According to the theory that I have ended up with, conscious minds exist as concepts in their own right. Further fungible instances of them also exist either as epiphenomenal realisations of interpretations of conceptual physics, or even more speculatively as epiphenomenal realisations of fundamental abstract or mathematical concepts that exist in their own right, and which also produce physical universes as epiphenomenal realisations. The greater abundance of certain concepts at each level of complexity is what gives rise to a greater abundance of ordered minds over disordered minds, and this helps to explain where we find ourselves as typical observers.

The conclusions from this chapter are arguably not as strong as some of the others that I have reached in this book, and I am not ruling out the possibility that objective physical reality exists in the way we normally think of it, with epiphenomenal minds dependent on it, but I find this less satisfactory and more problematic. By removing the superiority of physics over consciousness, we remove the threat of zombic materialism, and by embracing all possible conceptual existence, we remove the question of why things are this way rather than that, even though this would give rise to further problems, some of which I haven't begun to address, as I alluded to when discussing Max Tegmark's theory.

I said at the beginning that I do not solve the problem of consciousness in this book, so I hope you are not disappointed by the more speculative and less concrete (so to speak) conclusions in this final chapter. But I also hope that some readers will be encouraged to look in some of the directions that I have pointed towards and expand on some of these ideas. I look forward to reading your own work on the subject in the future.

Glossary

Access Consciousness – Ned Block's term for mental states that are accessible to us and can explicitly be referred to.

Anthropic Principle – The principle that any observations that we make must be compatible with the existence of observers. Anthropic reasoning is a class of reasoning where one reasons from the standpoint of one's own existence and position in the grand scheme of things.

Argument from Horse Racing – An argument, presented in this book, against the idea that causation in brains is relevant for producing consciousness. The argument is based on a thought experiment where neuronal firings could be rerouted and only allowed to reach their intended destination if the right combination of horses win their races, and the conclusion that there appears to be no clear line between a causally connected brain and a causally unconnected one.

As-If Intentionality – See **Derived Intentionality**.

Behaviourism – See **Logical Behaviourism**.

Biological Naturalism – John Searle's position that neither materialism nor dualism is correct.

Blindsight – The phenomenon by which some people can perform at above chance levels when guessing at what is happening in a part of their visual field where they are consciously blind.

Block Universe – The view of the whole of space-time from the outside as a static four-dimensional object.

Blockhead – A thought experiment by Ned Block where a being with no complex internal processing could have a look-up table with stock responses to every response in a conversation. This is an argument against logical behaviourism and against the idea behind the Turing Test.

Boltzmann Brain – A brain that appears fully formed due to random quantum fluctuations.

Brain in a Vat – A brain that is not connected to a body but instead is in a vat of nutrients. In thought experiments it is normally connected to a computer simulation of a world so that it has the experience that it is in a real body in a real world.

Cartesian Dualism – See **Substance Dualism**.

Cartesian Theatre – Daniel Dennett's idea (which he rejects) that there might be a central point in the brain where processing becomes conscious and where experience happens.

Causal Completeness of Physics – The position that every physical event has a physical cause and has no need of any non-physical explanation, such as a non-physical consciousness.

Causal Overdetermination – The phenomenon where a physical event has more than one sufficient cause.

Causation (also **Causality**) – The relationship between the causes and effects of events.

Chinese Nation – A thought experiment by Ned Block where everyone in China simulates the behaviour of a neuron. Block argues against functionalism by saying that such a 'brain' would not be conscious.

Chinese Room – A thought experiment by John Searle where he is inside a room and has a conversation in Chinese with someone outside the room despite understanding no Chinese himself. He is handed responses in Chinese through a hole and follows instructions (in English) on what to do with each response to come up with the next Chinese response himself. Searle argues that this blind symbol manipulation is equivalent to what happens in digital computers and uses this as an argument against functionalism and against the idea that digital computers can be conscious.

Compatibilism – The position that free will is compatible with determinism. See also **Free Will** and **Determinism**.

Consciousness – The subject matter of this book. To be conscious is to have subjective experiences and for there to be something it is like to be you.

Consciousness Delusion – The position that we have no valid reason to believe that we are conscious, so are deluded for doing so. The term borrows from Richard Dawkins. See also **Purpose Delusion** and **Zombic Materialism**.

Consciousness-Space-Time – The view of existence through time with respect to consciousness rather than physical existence, with beings that are more conscious taking up a larger area in consciousness-space than less conscious beings.

Corpus Callosum – A bundle of nerve fibres that connects the two hemispheres of the brain. See also **Split-Brain Patient**.

Derived Intentionality (also **As-If Intentionality**) – John Searle's term for intentionality that is not real, but only gains its meaning through an outside observer's interpretation. See also **Intrinsic Intentionality**.

Determinism – The position that every future event can be predicted from a complete knowledge of the present state of the universe.

Doomsday Argument – The argument that we should expect, statistically, to be somewhere in the middle of the ordering of all humans who have ever existed and who ever will exist, giving us an approximate prediction of when the human race will die out.

Dualism – The position that consciousness is non-physical and cannot be entirely explained by the laws of physics, meaning that there are two separate types of existence.

Easy Problems of Consciousness – David Chalmers's term for the purely physical problems of human brain functioning. See also **Hard Problem of Consciousness**.

Élan Vital – See **Vitalism**.

Eliminative Materialism (also **Eliminativism**) – The position that we are mistaken about some or all of our views of consciousness and that significant parts of our understanding will need to be replaced.

Epiphenomenal Gremlins – Daniel Dennett's argument that believing in an epiphenomenal consciousness is no better than believing that there are fourteen epiphenomenal gremlins in each cylinder of an internal combustion engine.

Epiphenomenalism – The dualistic position that consciousness has no effect in the physical world.

Experience Producer – A hypothetical module that attaches to one's brain to produce experiences of other conscious beings.

Explanatory Gap – Joseph Levine's term for the gap in understanding between the physical brain and consciousness.

Extended Mind – The position that our mind extends beyond the boundaries of the brain, into the body and possibly also into the environment.

Free Will – The ability to make a conscious choice that is both non-random and non-deterministic.

Functional Element – Under functionalism, this is the largest part of a functional system that can be replaced with a behaviourally identical part with no change in conscious experience.

Functionalism – The position that consciousness is determined by the internal functioning of a being and that if two beings were functionally equivalent but materially different, they would have the same conscious experiences. See also **Multiple Realisability**.

Fungibility – The interchangeability of objects. Two objects are fungible if they are identical in every way and cannot be said to have separate identities, such as two instances of £10 in your bank account.

Gödel's Incompleteness Theorem (the relevant part of) – That no formal system of generating mathematical proofs can prove all true statements of arithmetic.

Hard Problem of Consciousness – David Chalmers's term for the problem in determining how the physical workings of the brain can produce subjective experience, or consciousness. See also **Easy Problems of Consciousness**.

Higher-Order Thought (HOT) Theory – David Rosenthal's theory that a mental state is only conscious if there is a higher-order thought about it.

Idealism – The position that consciousness accounts for all existence and the physical world is just an illusion.

Identity Theory – The position that a conscious state is identical to a specific physical state.

Information Integration Theory of Consciousness – Giulio Tononi's theory that the amount of consciousness that a system has is determined by the amount of information that it can integrate. This measurement is known as Φ, or phi (the Greek letter).

Intentionality – What an object or mental state is about, its meaning or what it 'points to' in the real world.

Interactionist Dualism – The position that consciousness is not physical but can still causally influence the physical world.

Interpretationalism – My term for the position that consciousness is the realisation of an interpretation of a physical state.

Intrinsic Intentionality – John Searle's term for intentionality that requires no outside observer and the meaning of which is independent of anything else. See also **Derived Intentionality**.

Inverted Qualia – Conscious states that have been swapped with each other. The most common example is the inverted spectrum. For example, someone might experience green where you experience red and vice versa, with all the other corresponding changes.

Knowledge Argument – Frank Jackson's argument that Mary the Colour Scientist will learn something new when she sees colour for the first time, thus refuting materialism. See also **Mary the Colour Scientist**.

Kolmogorov Complexity – The number of characters it takes to specify an object within a particular system.

Logical Behaviourism – The position that everything about consciousness can be determined by behaviour. If two beings are behaviourally identical when presented with the same stimuli then they have the same conscious experience. See also **Turing Test.**

Mary the Colour Scientist – The main character in Frank Jackson's thought experiment. Mary understands everything about the neurophysiology of vision but has spent her life in a black and white room and has never seen any other colour. See also **Knowledge Argument.**

Materialism (also **Physicalism**) – The position that all existence is physical existence. If consciousness exists, then it is physical.

Mathematical Universe Hypothesis – Max Tegmark's theory that the physical universe is a mathematical structure.

Meta-Brain – A collection of neurons from many different brains that, when considered together, fire at the right times for an ordinary human brain.

Mind–Body Problem – The problem of how the physical body can produce the conscious mind.

Modal Realism – David Lewis's position that all possible physical universes exist concretely.

Monism – The position that there is only one fundamental type of existence, as opposed to the two in dualism. Materialism and idealism are monist theories.

Multiple Conscious Minds per Brain – The possibility that as a brain's functioning can be interpreted in more than one way, there might be more than one conscious mind associated with it. It can also refer to the separate possibility that there are many overlapping minds per brain.

Multiple Realisability – The position that a conscious state can be implemented by more than one type of physical state. See also **Functionalism.**

Neural Correlates of Consciousness – The neural events associated with a specific conscious experience.

Neutral Monism – A form of monism that asserts the primacy of neither the physical nor the conscious.

Non-Zombic Materialism – The position that materialism is true and that consciousness does exist, therefore consciousness is physical.

Ockham's Razor (also **Occam's Razor**) – The principle that you should favour the simplest hypothesis among competing options, all other things being equal.

Other Minds Problem – The problem that you cannot know that other people are conscious, as you cannot see their consciousness directly.

Panpsychism – The position that there is consciousness in everything, however small an amount.

Paradox of Phenomenal Judgement – The problem for epiphenomenalism that we consider ourselves to be conscious even though consciousness has no effect on our considerations and behaviour.

Personal Identity – The subject matter of the identity of conscious selves, including whether we remain the same entity over time as our bodies and brains change.

Phenomenal Mental States – Conscious mental states.

Physicalism – See **Materialism**.

Platonism – The position that abstract objects exist without having any physical or mental existence to anchor their existence.

Prarnt – The hypothetical robot, used in thought experiments in this book, that fully understands the physical human brain and is capable of drawing entirely objective conclusions.

Property Dualism – The dualistic position that consciousness is separate from the physical but is a property rather than a separate substance. See also **Substance Dualism.**

Protophenomenality – This refers to particles or states that are not conscious themselves but can be combined to create consciousness.

Psychological Mental States – David Chalmers's term for functional states within the brain that have physical effects and which may or may not be phenomenally conscious. The psychological states that correlate with phenomenal consciousness are collectively known as psychological consciousness.

Psychophysical Laws – Laws that determine the conscious states of physical things or processes.

Purpose Delusion – The position that as all physical laws and processes are blind, there is no purpose to any of our behaviour, and we are deluded into thinking that there is. The term borrows from Richard Dawkins. See also **Consciousness Delusion.**

Qualia (plural of **Quale**) – The individual states of consciousness, sometimes seen as elemental, such as the state of seeing red.

Random Brain – A hypothetical brain whose neurons are firing at random, used in thought experiments about the relationship between causation and consciousness.

Reference Class – The class of observers that you should consider yourself to be a sample from when reasoning anthropically.

Self-Consciousness – Consciousness of one's own self or of one's own consciousness.

Self – The possessor of a conscious experience or set of conscious experiences. See also **Personal Identity.**

Solipsism – The position that conscious minds other than yours do not exist.

Split-Brain Patient – A patient who has had their brain's two hemispheres separated by the severing of their corpus callosum. See also **Corpus Callosum.**

Strong Artificial Intelligence – John Searle's term for the position that digital computers can functionally replicate human brains and that these computers will also have the same consciousness as humans. See also **Weak Artificial Intelligence.**

Substance Dualism (also **Cartesian Dualism**) – The dualistic position that the physical and mental consist of two separate substances. See also **Property Dualism.**

Swampman – In Donald Davidson's thought experiment, Swampman is a being that forms at random after lightning hits a tree in swamp. This being is a molecule-for-molecule replica of Davidson and goes on to lead Davidson's life, after Davidson himself is reduced to his elements in the lightning strike.

Thought Experiment – An experiment that is performed mentally by taking an idea to its logical conclusions. Often this is because an experiment cannot be physically conducted for whatever reason.

Turing Test – Alan Turing's test for whether a machine can think by seeing if it can successfully mimic human output to the point where someone cannot reliably distinguish between the machine's and a human's responses. See also **Logical Behaviourism.**

Universalism – Arnold Zuboff's theory that there is only one self.

Unity of Consciousness – The idea that our conscious thoughts are connected together in one unified self.

Vitalism – The outdated idea that life cannot be explained by physical means but requires the force of life, or élan vital.

Weak Artificial Intelligence – John Searle's term for the position that digital computers can functionally replicate human brains but that these computers will not be conscious. See also **Strong Artificial Intelligence.**

Zombic Materialism – The position that we are all zombies – that materialism is true and consciousness does not exist.

Zombie – A hypothetical being that is functionally identical to a human being but without consciousness.

References

Blackmore, Susan. 2005. *Conversations on Consciousness.* Oxford: Oxford University Press.

Block, Ned. 1978. 'Troubles with functionalism.' *Minnesota Studies in the Philosophy of Science*, 9, pp. 261–325.

Block, Ned. 1995. 'On a confusion about a function of consciousness.' *Behavioral and Brain Sciences*, 18 (2), pp. 227–247.

Block, Ned. 1981. 'Psychologism and behaviorism.' *Philosophical Review*, 90, pp. 5–43.

Bostrom, Nick. 2002. *Anthropic Bias: Observation Selection Effects in Science and Philosophy.* New York: Routledge.

Carter, Rita. 2002. *Consciousness.* London: Weidenfeld & Nicolson.

Chalmers, David. 1996. *The Conscious Mind: In Search of a Fundamental Theory.* Oxford: Oxford University Press.

Chalmers, David. 2010. *The Character of Consciousness.* Oxford: Oxford University Press

Churchland, Paul. 1981. 'Eliminative materialism and the propositional attitudes.' *Journal of Philosophy*, 78 (2), pp. 67–90.

Churchland, Paul. 1989. 'Knowing qualia: a reply to Jackson.' In *A Neuro-computational Perspective: The Nature of Mind and the Structure of Science*, pp. 67–76. Cambridge, MA: MIT Press.

Clark, Andy. 2008. *Supersizing the Mind: Embodiment, Action and Cognitive Extension.* New York: Oxford University Press.

Clark, Andy & Chalmers, David. 1998. 'The extended mind.' *Analysis*, 58 (1), pp. 7–19.

Davidson, Donald. 1987. 'Knowing one's own mind.' *Proceedings of the American Philosophical Association*, 60, pp. 441–458.

Dawkins, Richard. 1998. *Unweaving the Rainbow.* London: Penguin.

Dawkins, Richard. 2006. *The God Delusion.* London: Bantam Press.

Dennett, Daniel. 1988. 'Quining qualia.' In A. Marcel & E. Bisiach (eds), *Consciousness in Contemporary Science*, pp. 42–77. Oxford: Oxford University Press.

Dennett, Daniel. 1991. *Consciousness Explained*. Boston and New York: Little, Brown.

Dennett, Daniel. 1995. 'The unimagined preposterousness of zombies.' *Journal of Consciousness Studies*, 2 (4), pp. 322–326.

Dennett, Daniel. 1996a. *Kinds of Minds: Towards an Understanding of Consciousness*. London: Weidenfeld & Nicolson.

Dennett, Daniel. 1996b. 'Cow-sharks, magnets and swampman.' *Mind and Language*, 11 (1), pp. 76–77.

Dennett, Daniel. 2005. *Sweet Dreams: Philosophical Obstacles to a Science of Consciousness*. Cambridge, MA: MIT Press.

Deutsch, David. 2012. *The Beginning of Infinity: Explanations that Transform the World*. London: Penguin Books.

Fodor, Jerry. 1975. *The Language of Thought*. Cambridge, MA: Harvard University Press.

Gazzaniga, Michael & LeDoux, Joseph. 1978. *The Integrated Mind*. New York: Plenum Press.

Gallup, Gordon, Jr. 1970. 'Chimpanzees: self recognition'. *Science*, 167, pp. 86–87.

Hameroff, Stuart & Penrose, Roger. 1996. 'Orchestrated reduction of quantum coherence in brain microtubules: a model for consciousness?' In S.R. Hameroff, A.W. Kaszniak & A.C. Scott (eds), *Toward a Science of Consciousness – The First Tucson Discussions and Debates*, pp. 507–540. Cambridge, MA: MIT Press.

Hirstein, William. 2012. 'Conjoined twins, conjoined brains, but conjoined minds?: How two little girls may shed light on an age-old mystery.' Retrieved on 10th March 2014, from http://www.psychologytoday.com/blog/mindmelding/201207/conjoined-twins-conjoined-brains-conjoined-minds

Hofstadter, Douglas. 1979. *Gödel, Escher, Bach: An Eternal Golden Braid*. New York: Basic Books.

Hofstadter, Douglas. 1981a. 'Reflections.' In D.R. Hofstadter & D.C. Dennett (eds), *The Mind's I: Fantasies and Reflections on Self and Soul*, pp. 373–382. New York: Basic Books.

Hofstadter, Douglas. 1981b. 'A Conversation with Einstein's Brain.' In D.R. Hofstadter & D.C. Dennett (eds), *The Mind's I: Fantasies and Reflections on Self and Soul*, pp. 430–457. New York: Basic Books.

Hofstadter, Douglas & Dennett, Daniel (eds). 1981a. *The Mind's I: Fantasies and Reflections on Self and Soul*. New York: Basic Books.

Hofstadter, Douglas & Dennett, Daniel. 1981b. 'Reflections.' In D.R. Hofstadter & D.C. Dennett (eds), *The Mind's I: Fantasies and Reflections on*

Self and Soul, pp. 212–213. New York: Basic Books.

Jackson, Frank. 1982. 'Epiphenomenal qualia.' *Philosophical Quarterly*, 32, 127, pp. 127–136.

Jackson, Frank. 1986. 'What Mary didn't know.' *The Journal of Philosophy*, 83 (5), pp. 291–295.

Koch, Christof. 2012. *Consciousness: Confessions of a Romantic Reductionist*. Cambridge, MA: MIT Press.

Levine, Joseph. 1983. 'Materialism and qualia: the explanatory gap.' *Pacific Philosophical Quarterly*, 64, pp. 354–361.

Lewis, David. 1986. *On the Plurality of Worlds*. Oxford: Blackwell Publishing.

Moody, Todd. 1994. 'Conversations with zombies.' *Journal of Consciousness Studies*, 1 (2), pp. 196–200.

Nagel, Thomas. 1974. 'What is it like to be a bat?' *Philosophical Review*, 83 (4), pp. 435–450.

Noë, Alva. 2009. *Out of Our Heads: Why You Are Not Your Brain, and Other Lessons from the Biology of Consciousness*. New York: Hill and Wang.

Papineau, David & Selina, Howard. 2000. *Introducing Consciousness*. Cambridge: Icon Books.

Parfit, Derek. 2002. 'Reductionism and personal identity.' In D.J. Chalmers (ed.), *Philosophy of Mind: Classical and Contemporary Readings*, pp. 655–661.

Penrose, Roger. 1989. *The Emperor's New Mind: Concerning Computers, Minds, and the Laws of Physics*. New York: Oxford University Press.

Penrose, Roger. 1994. *Shadows of the Mind: A Search for the Missing Science of Consciousness*. New York: Oxford University Press.

Penrose, Roger. 1996. 'Beyond the doubting of a shadow: a reply to commentaries on *Shadows of the Mind*.' Retrieved on 10th March 2014, from http://www.calculemus.org/MathUniversalis/NS/10/01penrose.html

Poundstone, William. 1988. *Labyrinths of Reason: Paradox, Puzzles, and the Frailty of Knowledge*. New York: Anchor Books.

Putnam, Hilary. 1981. *Reason, Truth and History*. Cambridge: Cambridge University Press.

Ramsey, William. 2013. 'Eliminative materialism'. In E.N. Zalta (ed.), *The Stanford Encyclopedia of Philosophy (Summer 2013 Edition)*, Retrieved on 10th March 2014, from http://plato.stanford.edu/archives/sum2013/entries/materialism-eliminative/

Risse, Gail & Gazzaniga, Michael. 1976. 'Verbal retrieval of right hemisphere memories established in the absence of language.' *Neurology*, 26, p. 354.

Rosenthal, David. 2002. 'Explaining consciousness'. In D.J. Chalmers (ed.), *Philosophy of Mind: Classical and Contemporary Readings*, pp. 406–421. Oxford: Oxford University Press.

Searle, John. 1981. 'Minds, brains, and programs.' In D.R. Hofstadter & D.C. Dennett (eds), *The Mind's I: Fantasies and Reflections on Self and Soul*, pp. 353–373. New York: Basic Books.

Searle, John. 1992. 'Breaking the hold: silicon brains, conscious robots, and other minds.' In *The Rediscovery of the Mind*. Cambridge, MA: MIT Press.

Searle, John. 1998. *The Mystery of Consciousness*. London: Granta Publications.

Slezak, Michael. 2013. 'The now delusion: do past, present and future exist only in our heads?' *New Scientist*, 220 (2941), pp. 34–38.

Smullyan, Raymond. 1981. 'An unfortunate dualist.' In D.R. Hofstadter & D.C. Dennett (eds), *The Mind's I: Fantasies and Reflections on Self and Soul*, pp. 383–384. New York: Basic Books.

Strawson, Galen. 1998, 2011. 'Free will.' In E. Craig (ed.), *Routledge Encyclopedia of Philosophy*. London: Routledge. Retrieved on 10th March 2014, from http://www.rep.routledge.com/article/V014

Tegmark, Max. 2008. 'The mathematical universe.' *Foundations of Physics*, 38, pp. 101–150.

Tegmark, Max. 2014. *Our Mathematical Universe: My Quest for the Ultimate Nature of Reality*. London: Allen Lane.

Tononi, Giulio. 2007. 'The information integration theory of consciousness.' In M. Velmans and S. Schneider (eds), *The Blackwell Companion to Consciousness*, pp. 287–299. Oxford: Blackwell Publishing Ltd.

Tononi, Giulio. 2012. *Phi: A Voyage from the Brain to the Soul*. New York: Pantheon Books.

Turing, Alan. 1950. 'Computing machinery and intelligence.' *Mind*, 59 (236), pp. 433–460.

Zuboff, Arnold. 1981. 'The story of a brain.' In D.R. Hofstadter & D.C. Dennett (eds), *The Mind's I: Fantasies and Reflections on Self and Soul*, pp. 202–212. New York: Basic Books.

Zuboff, Arnold. 1990. 'One self: the logic of experience.' *Inquiry*, 33, pp. 39–68.

Zuboff, Arnold. 1994. 'What is a mind?' *Midwest Studies in Philosophy*, 19, pp. 183–205.

Zuboff, Arnold. 2000. 'The perspectival nature of probability and inference.' *Inquiry*, 43, pp. 353–358.

Index

Index

www.ingramcontent.com/pod-product-compliance
Lightning Source LLC
Chambersburg PA
CBHW052145070326
40689CB00050B/2057